Hoping,

Healing, &

Whole-ish

Finding Restoration in the Midst of Brokenness

By Mariah Miller

ISBN: 978-0-578-98718-7

TABLE OF CONTENTS

To my Granny, the original author in the family. Thank you for being an incredible example of faith, service, and love. I miss you, but I know I'll see you again one day.

To all those I love who are broken but will be restored. Know that you are loved even now.

Download your FREE BOOKLET today!

You'll get:

- Reflection questions to go with each chapter
- BONUS videos, songs, and authors to inspire you even more
- Access to an exclusive Facebook community
- A beautiful layout you can use on your device or print for yourself

Use the questions to reflect on your own healing journey as you read the book. Discuss them with a friend over coffee, journal about them, or whatever suits your fancy. And enjoy all the little jewels of extra inspiration as you go!

Don't miss out! Download FREE at:

www.hopinghealingandwholeish.com

INTRODUCTION

When I first came across kintsugi pottery, I asked myself, "Is it broken or is it restored?"

The process of kintsugi pottery is from the Japanese word meaning "gold joinery." This art form takes fractured vessels and glues them back together using lacquer mixed with gold dust.[1] It takes what is broken and makes it whole again without trying to hide that it was once broken. And that's what resonated with me.

I am that broken pot.

There are pieces of my heart too shattered and too small to be glued back together, but God fills those empty spaces. He is the glue that binds my broken pieces back together. That space created in my brokenness is exactly where miracles happen. It's where The Light gets in.

As I write this, my season of life has been one of hoping, healing, and finding wholeness. And much like kintsugi, I've learned the process must happen in that order. I must find hope for a better future, for restoration, for my heart. Only then will I be willing to seek healing and hand over my broken pieces to God. Then He can take those broken pieces and make me whole, make me new.

God is close when we are brokenhearted (Ps. 34:17-18), like a potter gets close to the vessel he's working on to make something beautiful and restore what's been broken. Each piece of pottery is unique, with its own cracks to be filled. The same is true of you and I. We have different hurts, traumas, failures, losses, and heartbreaks that all need to be filled with God's grace and love.

In kintsugi, repairs are made in a few different ways. You can fill the cracks, fill the space left by an entire missing piece, or even combine pieces from two different broken vessels.[2] There may be cracks in our lives that are filled pretty quickly or easily. But some damage leaves bigger holes, pieces of us we won't get back. Those places must be filled completely by God's hand, and this will take time, patience and trust. And sometimes God takes broken pieces of other people and uses them to heal us. This requires complete surrender of our most broken parts and the willingness to let God make something new out of us.

If we withhold our broken pieces, we will not find wholeness. As you read this book, I encourage you to lay down the broken pieces, despite your fear or discomfort, one page at a time, one story at a time, so that God can make you whole.

The bigger the crack or missing piece, the more space there is for beautiful gold to fill it. Don't be afraid of the "big cracks," the stuff that feels too big to ever get over or too sensitive to ever bring up.

That's the place where God does His most beautiful work.

The kintsugi piece is never considered unsalvageable. Instead it is understood to be *more beautiful* for being broken.[3] It becomes known for its magnificent restoration, not the damage it suffered. Instead of trying to camouflage the broken pieces, kintsugi seeks to make beauty from them. If it were put back together with clear glue trying to hide the cracks, it still wouldn't look whole or even as good as it once did. But if those cracks are filled with gold, bringing attention to the brokenness on purpose, it not only becomes whole again but becomes even more beautiful than before. In fact, these "broken" vessels become more valuable than the originals.

God wants to take all of your broken pieces and turn them into something even more beautiful and valuable than who you once were. You are a treasure in a jar of clay (2 Cor. 4:7), a pile of broken pieces ready to be made beautiful and whole.

The miraculous things Jesus does in our healing process are the gold that rejoins our broken pieces, the light that shines through the cracks. Each time He sends you a scripture at the right moment, a song that lifts your spirits, a sermon that speaks to you, a person in your life to share the truth you need to hear, or a dream that gives you hope again, He's filling your dark places with light and gluing your broken pieces back together until you're whole.

I pray the stories of hope, healing, and wholeness we're going to explore in this book will serve as glue for your soul. Because when you begin hoping, you can begin healing. When you begin healing, you can become whole again. You may be whole-ish now, just trying to hold the pieces

> You may be whole-ish now, just trying to hold the pieces together, but that's not how you have to stay.

together, but that's not how you have to stay. If you let Him, God will take your broken pieces and put them back together one by one until your whole-ish becomes wholeness.

In his letter to the Galations, Paul says, "All that matters now is living in the faith that works and expresses itself through love" (Gal. 5:6).[4] This book is an act of that faith, and I hope you feel that it's an expression of love. The God who is renewing my hope, healing my wounds, and making me whole, can do the same for you. God is the Potter molding us, the Writer of our stories, and the Lover of our souls. He is making beauty from the ashes of the past.

"You See My Heart"

*God, you're like a magnifying
glass to my heart;*

*You see it all no matter how well I
try to hide it.*

*You see that ugly patch I tried to
sew on to cover all those sinful
stains.*

*You watch as I try to stop the
crack from growing and fail
without the necessary glue.*

*You watch as that hole created by
my loss consumes me and is never
satisfied.*

*You see where the piece I gave
away once was and the guilt it has
wrought on my soul.*

*You see each chip taken out that I
pretended not to feel.*

*You see every scab and wound
that I do my best to heal.*

*No glue, no tape, no medicine, no
patch, could ever fix the damage
done to my heart.*

*Only You, God, who see the root
and the source,*

*Can heal the wounds with your
most precious love.*

*No matter the ache, no matter the
pain, all I have to do is call on
Your name.*

*Poem by me at age 17
(don't judge!)*

PIECES OF HOPE

I see you like a beautiful, handcrafted, ceramic vessel. Your value is in how rare, unique, and purposefully designed you are. But you've been through a lot. You've had a few hard bumps. Some little falls. And some big drops. You want to look and function like you did before. Before you were broken. Before life broke your heart.

A part of you is in pieces. Pieces that don't seem like they'll ever go back together. Pieces that you don't want anyone to notice lying on the floor. Pieces. That's all they'll ever be.

But you are not broken forever. That is if you will lay down the broken pieces of yourself and let God pick them up one by one. He knows how they fit back together.

You are not discarded or damaged. You were designed for a purpose, and you will be strengthened for it again. God doesn't need new material. He starts with the pieces.

So it's time to gather up the pieces of your broken heart. The ones that slid under the cabinet or were hidden away in a box. Don't leave a single one behind. Lay them all on the table.

Then watch as God restores your hope and shows you something beautiful can be made from this broken mess.

CHAPTER 1:

HELPLESS TO HEAL

2 Kings 4:8-37 [1]

Desperate. Disappointed. And determined to move on. That's how we find the Shunammite woman. You may have never heard her story before, but it's one I certainly relate to. She's stopped asking for the one thing she wanted most, a child. Her husband is old, and they haven't been able to have a child. But she's determined not to sit in disappointment or anger.

She notices the prophet Elisha comes through town often. She can't help it. She's the woman who likes to take care of others, so she offers to feed him when he passes through on his journey. Her food must have been good, because he keeps coming back.

One day she walks up to the empty room on top of her house, the one she'd hoped would be for a child one day, and decides it's time to use it for something else. She and her husband go to IKEA, get some furniture for Elisha, and set him up a spot to stay.

It amazes me that she's willing to sacrifice in the midst of her disappointment. It amazes me all the more that God wasn't just watching her and clapping, saying, "you go girl." Her sacrifice in that season of disappointment not only glorified Him and helped others, it opened doors for Him to move closer to her as we're about to see. God didn't forget to book Elisha an AirBnB on his way to where He told him to go. God sent Elisha to bring a miracle to the woman who had given up on one ever happening.

On one of his regular visits to her house Elisha decides he really wants to do something in return for all she's done for him. He says, "You have gone to all this trouble for us. Now what can be done for you? Can we speak to the king for you?" (2 Kings 4:13). She responds like many of us do, who have lost hope for the one thing we desire most.

All she says is, "I have a home among my own people," basically, "I'm fine." The earthly powers that wanted to help her were never going to be able to meet her truest desires. No one could. So why bother asking?

God saw what she was doing for everyone else and wanted to bless her. It's why He sent the relentless Elisha who wasn't taking "I'm fine" as an answer. Elisha stopped *asking her* what she wanted and started *asking God* what could be done for her.

You need people in your life who look for ways to bless you even when you say you're fine, even when you've stopped hoping for more. In her case, Elisha's servant Gehazi, noticed her need and went to bat for her when she wasn't even aware of it. He's the one that points out to Elisha that she has a husband who's not getting younger and still has no child.

Elisha calls her up to the room she'd converted for him to stay in, and she stands in the doorway. Maybe she thinks he just wants another slice of pie, but instead he makes her an emotional promise. He tells her, "About this time next year, you will hold a son in your arms" (v.16). That deep, wounded place in her heart must have cracked open hearing that. She objects immediately and says, "No! Don't mislead your servant!"

> ...even when you've given up on it altogether, God is orchestrating miracles.

I totally sympathize with where she's at. She's too scared she'll only be disappointed again. She doesn't even want to believe the promise coming out of his mouth. That's how we feel about promises in our lives that are too emotional to think about. They're hard to hear at times and even harder to hope for. We think the deepest desires we have are impossible at this point and yet we're still hoping for them because God put them in our hearts. It's like being torn apart.

The very next words are, "but she became pregnant" (v.17). We don't know how she felt or where her faith was over that next year. I wonder if she would get her hopes up some days only to turn around and be scared to death the next. As she waited, I wonder if she told anyone else or was too afraid to even say the words out loud. Either way, God worked, despite her fear and doubt. The very next year the unthinkable happened; she had a son, just like Elisha promised her.

You may be going about your life doing the best you can or even trying to allow God space in your life, but it's likely there's also a buried dream or desire that you're too hurt to even hope for anymore. Maybe you feel unappreciated by those you're sacrificing for, misunderstood by those who claim they're close to you, or just plain alone.

Even then, even when you don't expect it, and even when you've given up on it altogether, God is orchestrating miracles.

God's pursuit of us is relentless and His goodness endless. So don't be afraid when it seems all hope is lost, because "if God always met your expectations, He'd never have the opportunity to exceed them."[2]

🔁🔁🔁

If you've ever watched a TV drama, you know the plot of a seemingly lovely story can turn dark really quickly, usually right before a commercial break!

That's exactly what happens with the Shunammite woman's story.

She has a son she never thought she'd have. As she watches him grow and play her heart bursts with joy and a love she thought she'd never know. But then the plot turns dark. The boy grows until one day he goes out to his father in the field screaming that he has a headache. Dad is too old to carry him, so he tells a servant to carry him to his mother.

Her husband had to feel helpless in that moment. And so must have the woman as she held her son as long as she could. Before the sun set, the boy died, but her faith didn't.

As hard as it must have been to move, she took immediate action. She carried his lifeless body upstairs and laid him on the bed Elisha slept in, the bed that was supposed to be her son's as he grew up. Then she closed the door.

It had to be hard to lay down his body. I can only imagine, she wanted to hold onto him longer. Maybe she felt guilty for leaving him, but in the end she knew that if she didn't let go of him she couldn't help him. I know what it's like to walk away in pain because I felt it was the only way to bring healing to someone in pain. That doesn't mean the whispers of guilt or fear aren't there.

She doesn't say much to anyone, including her husband. She just tells him she's going to find Elisha and needs a servant and a donkey. He must have thought she was nuts because he says, "Why go today? It's not a holiday."

Maybe he felt like there wasn't a point in trying anymore. Maybe he felt it wouldn't be important enough to the man of God, or maybe she hadn't told him what she was trying to do. All he gets in response is, "It's all right" and she takes off. The distance from Shunaam to Mount Carmel (where Elisha was) is about twenty miles one way. That's a long journey on a donkey, and it was likely through a valley. Yet, despite the distance and discomfort, nothing was going to stop her from seeking out the only one who could help.

When she gets close to the mountain, Gehazi goes out to her first and asks if she's ok and if her family is ok. Once again, she says, "Everything's alright". Maybe she didn't want to tell him the deep battle she was in. Maybe she truly believed God was working it out. Maybe she just didn't want to take her problems to someone who couldn't do anything about it. Or maybe she thought she had to be strong for those who were depending on her.

No matter what, she knew everything wasn't alright, and she had to take it directly to the man of God.

Elisha sees her when she is a long way off. And as soon as she gets to him, she falls at his feet and grabs onto them. Gehazi tries to stop her, but Elisha tells him to back off. All she manages to get out is, "Did I ask you for a son, my lord? Didn't I tell you, 'Don't raise my hopes?'" (v.28).

She's angry and confused because she got what she wanted most, what she'd given up on, and now it's been taken away. I get that feeling. When we lose someone or something in our lives, we are tempted to ask why God gave it to us at all? Wouldn't it have been easier to never have the blessing in the first place? If ignorance is bliss, why give us our desires only to take them away? Surely this is not what we asked for.

What I love is that she poured out her pain and disappointment openly. The Shunammite woman didn't waste time blaming her husband or stopping to ask her neighbors for prayer. She let go of what she couldn't control and held firmly to what she knew.

Verse 27 says God hid what was wrong from Elisha. I wonder if that was because if Elisha had known what was wrong he would have gone to the house already, and she wouldn't have had to seek God out for her miracle. It's hard to understand the purpose in our pain sometimes, but God has a reason behind how He reveals His answers. He sends help at the right time.

🯅🯅🯅

Elisha, probably desperate to help the woman as quickly as he could, sends Gehazi ahead of them with his staff to try and heal the boy. If she was willing to stay with Elisha no matter what, she may have accepted that physical healing for her son might not be God's plan. But she wasn't settling for human intervention. She knew she needed divine intervention from the prophet of God-Elisha, and she wasn't going home without him.

This mother believed God would bring healing in some way or she wouldn't have stayed with Elisha at all. She would have been at home mourning with her family. Her faith, and maybe even desperation, must have moved Elisha because he got up and followed her back home. As she holds onto Elisha and makes the long march home, Gehazi comes running back to tell them the staff didn't work. How crushing that must have been to any hope she still had. Yet she keeps walking home, trusting she'd see the miracle anyway.

She takes Elisha up to the room where the boy lies, and he shuts the door behind him. This mom probably thought she'd get to go in with him, maybe tell him the situation, or see what he was doing. But instead, here she stands at the same door where Elisha had promised her a son a few years ago. She's at the doorstep of her dreams, and all she can do is wait. She's pacing, praying, trying not to let the consolation of her family and friends deter her from having faith.

She has to fight the temptation to open the door just a crack or knock on it. As women, we want to help and fix things for those we love, but we also must stand outside the door and wait when it's required. That's the true test—waiting. It's not recorded in scripture that the woman even asked Elisha to raise her son to life. Maybe she didn't know if she could find the faith to ask for the impossible. She just knew God was her only hope.

Behind closed doors, Elisha lays down on top of the boy, "mouth to mouth, eyes to eyes, hands to hands" (v. 34). The first time the boy's body only gets warm. But Elisha doesn't give up. He lays on him one more time. Maybe it was the mom's pleading running through his mind that made him try one more time.

He's so close he's breathing on the boy, and the boy sneezes seven times (a sign of completion in scripture) and opens his eyes. Elisha sends for the mom, so she must have not had her ear pressed to the door. Or at least she pretended not to be frantically listening just outside the room. Elisha puts her son back in her arms. She falls at his feet in worship, just like she did when she thought all was lost.

When God brought her a son, there was only one verse about the miracle, and only one or two when he's brought back to life. There are thirty verses that talk about her process before and after those two miracles. God must have been more focused on her faith than the miracle itself.

When we get desperate and take what little faith we have to God, He is moved. As Craig Groeschel says, "We don't have to know God's plans to trust

God's purposes."³ He'll give us hope to cast out fear if we'll let Him.

You may have felt helpless to heal yourself , to heal the one you love most, or to protect others in your life from pain. You may know what it's like to comfort those in pain in your life and be comforted by them until you can't hold on anymore. Someone pushes you away or simply lets go, and it doesn't matter that you *want* to hold on. When those seasons come, we can't let bitterness, loneliness, or abandonment set in. We must recognize we're at the end of what we can do and it's time for healing only God can do.

> Until we're willing to close the door and let Him work, nothing will change.

That's when we have to close the door in faith, and trust Jesus to heal the places where we're most helpless and hopeless. He needs to be alone with the person we love who's in pain or left alone with a problem that's too big for us to handle. Until we're willing to close the door and let Him work, nothing will change.

It's so hard to leave things behind closed doors so God can work. But we can trust that while we wait outside the doors, God is working in us and those we love. The healing process is a personal one that requires God to get close to us, but we can't stop when the journey to our healing or the healing of those we love is uncomfortable and requires going through a valley.

I have no idea how my journey will end up, how long certain doors will be closed, or how long healing will take. But I pray God leads me through the valley to help and comfort. I pray God won't let either of us give up hope when we're weary or uncomfortable because there is healing on the other side of this.

God is watching for us in the distance, like the prodigal son coming home. Even when we're a long way off from our healing, he's listening for the humble, desperate pleas of his people. In our seasons of brokenness and pain, we have to cling to his promises and lay it all at his feet. Don't let anyone push you away from your pursuit of Him. He knows the pain of our hearts, when we're helpless to fix ourselves, He is orchestrating healing.

No matter how long it takes, God won't give up on our healing. His power, that raised this boy to life, is working miracles in our hearts, our situations, and our relationships. Neither the mom nor the son are named in this passage, yet their story of healing is a message of hope for us. One day your story of healing will restore someone else because He will finish what He started in you.

Look at the Pieces:

What dream or desire have you given up hope on? What do you need to do to take that disappointment or anger you carry to his feet?

- What miracles have you experienced in your past that could be fuel for your hope today?

- Who or what has God sent into your life to reignite your hope? Are you inviting them in or pushing them away?

Prayer: *Jesus, I know you see my darkest disappointment and the hopes I've tried to bury. I pray you give me the courage to honestly lay those broken pieces of myself at your feet in faith that you are still in the business of miracles. Just like you did for this mom, I know you will resurrect dead things in my life, starting with the hope I've lost. When I can't do anything to heal myself or those I love most, work behind closed doors. In waiting seasons when the doors seem closed, give me faith to keep trusting. As you work healing in my life, use my story to bring healing to others. Thank you for the miracles You've already put in motion that I can't see yet.*

Chapter 2:

Praising in Hoping

1 Samuel 1-2:11 1; Psalm 69 2

In recent years there has been a lot of talk about infertility. In today's world there are often treatments to help with that and doctors to explain what's going on. Maybe you know someone or are someone who's dealt with the struggle of infertility. In 1 Samuel 1, we find a woman named Hannah who is in that same boat except there are no fertility doctors, no explanations, and no treatments to help.

Year after year, Hannah, her husband, and his other wife (oh yea, there's that!) went up to the temple to make a sacrifice. When it came time to eat the meat from the sacrifice, every year her husband, Elkanah, would give her a double portion "because he loved her" (1:5). But that didn't make up for what she was lacking.

Hannah was loved and blessed with a "double portion" *before* she got the child she prayed for (v. 5). However, it probably didn't feel that way as she

15

watched her husband's other wife have multiple children. Elkanah loved her and must have felt helpless to give her the one thing he knew she wanted most. Every night when he tucked in one of his children, maybe a part of him felt guilty that Hannah had no one to tuck in. He tried to make up for it in other ways, but still she looked angry, sad, desperate, and confused.

All the while, Elkanah's other wife provoked her by pointing out her deficiency over and over. Sometimes we experience this in our lives, whether it's another person, a circumstance, or our own voice of self-doubt. That constant poking can convince us to give up hope, but Hannah persisted.

When they go to the temple this particular year, Hannah's heart comes to a boiling point. The whole family has already made their sacrifice and eaten their meal, but Hannah goes back to pray again.

"In her deep anguish Hannah prayed to the Lord, weeping bitterly." (v. 10). All those anxious thoughts she's had about "what if I don't ever have a child," the lying voices that whispered to her "you're not enough," and the countless nights of crying herself to sleep all come out before the Lord.

"The Lord had closed her womb" (v.5). God was the one who had created this void in her life! Yet she doesn't even ask why this time. She just pleads with him saying, "if you will only look upon your servant's misery and remember me, and not forget your servant but give her a son, then I will give him to the Lord for all the days of his life" (v. 11).

Her prayer wasn't about getting answers or simply getting what she wanted. It was about God getting the glory in her life. Prayer isn't about us gaining control but keeping our eyes on the One who *is* in control.

As Hannah prays in her heart, no one can hear her, but Eli the priest is watching her. Eli just sees what appears to be a drunk lady talking to herself and comes over to see what's going on. Hannah explains that she's "deeply troubled," "in great anguish and grief," and was just "pouring out her soul to the Lord" (v. 15-16). Other translations call her "a woman troubled in spirit."

She had an internal battle going on just to keep clinging to hope. No one saw it or understood it except the Lord. Notice, Hannah never tells Eli what she's upset about or praying about, but God answers her prayer through Eli anyway. Eli tells her, "Go in peace, and may God grant you what you've asked of him". She answers, "May your servant find favor in your eyes" (v. 17-18).

> **Prayer isn't about us gaining control but keeping our eyes on the One who *is* in control.**

Her response is about more than her words though. The moment she leaves the temple she already has that peace he promised. She goes about her day, eats, and doesn't look sad anymore. She had no child yet, not even a timeline about when she would get one. That's a peace that only comes from hope placed firmly in the hands of the Father.

When they got back home, she and Elkanah got busy, and the Lord remembered his promise to her. She felt forgotten when she was praying back at the temple, but God doesn't forget His promises to us. And "in due time" she gave birth to a son, named Samuel (v. 20).

This miracle did not happen on her time table. In fact we wouldn't have labeled Hannah as favored by God earlier in the story, because for years and years she didn't have a child. But God's favor comes in God's timing or it *wouldn't* be favor. We wouldn't be ready for what He wants to give us.

Samuel's name means "God heard me," which shows us Hannah didn't forget where her miracle came from. I wonder if God had answered her much earlier if her perspective would have been different.

Hannah's story wasn't over when she got her miracle. When Samuel was weaned, she made good on her promise to the Lord. She surrendered the most precious thing to her, Samuel, in service at the temple all the rest of his life. Instead of getting to watch him grow up, she would get to visit him once a year when they went back to the temple. She explains her sacrifice by saying, "I have lent him to the Lord"

(v. 28). That is the definition of holding what God gives us with open hands.

> Sometimes we have to get desperate enough, troubled enough, anxious enough, or confused enough to truly press into God in prayer.

Sometimes we have to get desperate enough, troubled enough, anxious enough, or confused enough to truly press into God in prayer. We've all been there. Others around you may notice some of the signs, but don't really know what's going on internally or how to help. God will send us people in our season of desperate hope who may not know what we need, but He will use them to help us anyway.

🪔🪔🪔

Hannah's song of praise in 1 Samuel 2 speaks beautifully to her journey from desperation to hope again. David echoes that song in one of his own in Psalm 69:

> *These floods of trouble have risen*
> *higher and higher... I'm about to*
> *drown in this storm. I'm weary,*
> *exhausted with weeping... and I'm*
> *waiting for you, God, to come*
> *through for me...*

Must I restore what I never took away?...

Nothing within me is hidden from your sight!

But I KEEP calling out to you, Yahweh! I know you will bend down to listen to me, for now is the season of favor. Because of your faithful love for me, your answer to my prayer will be my sure salvation.

Pull me out of this mess... Rescue me... Don't let this flood drown me. Save me... Oh, Lord God, answer my prayers! I need to see your tender kindness, your grace, your compassion, and your constant love. Just let me see your face, and turn your heart toward me. Come running quickly to your servant. In this deep distress, come and answer my prayer. Come closer as a friend and redeem me. Set me free...

They dishonor me with shame and disgrace... You know, Lord, what I'm going through, and you see it all. I'm heartsick and heartbroken by it all.

I am burdened and broken by this pain. When your miracle rescue

> *comes to me, it will lift me to the*
> *highest place.*
>
> *My praises mean more to you than*
> *my gifts and sacrifices... All who*
> *seek you will see God do this for*
> *them, and they'll overflow with*
> *gladness... Yahweh does listen to*
> *the poor and needy and will not*
> *abandon his prisoners of love...*
> *God will come to save.*

That waiting season where you're not sure how much longer you can hang on, feels like you're drowning, like you can't keep your head above water. It is a special kind of frustration and helplessness when the pain or loss you feel isn't your fault, and yet you can't fix it or bring them back. Hannah and Elkanah both knew a version of that.

And yet even in that painful waiting and hoping, God sees all of us. He knows how we got here. He knows what broken pieces need healing. We must have faith to keep calling out to God, trusting He will respond, like Hannah's wailing at the temple. Clinging to hope in the waiting isn't always pretty, but it's the only thing that works.

> ... even in that painful waiting and hoping, God sees all of us.

No matter what storm we've been in, our season of favor and hope can begin right *now* because God's love is here with us. His timing may not be our timing, but because He loves us His timing will always be right. Hannah didn't like the years that went by where she wasn't having children, but it doesn't mean they were years without God's favor on her. He knew where her story was going, knew the blessings coming, before she ever saw the positive pregnancy test.

Holding onto hope when we're broken and need help requires that we cry out in desperate ways. But it's in those desperate, broken spaces we see God's grace and love fill in the gaps and put us back together. God must draw close to us to heal us and set us free. He can't pick up our broken pieces if we keep Him at arm's length.

If we get so focused on the mess of our broken pieces, we'll let shame set in. We'll be broken and need help, but be terrified that others will see through our cracks. God didn't leave Hannah alone in her shame, and he doesn't leave us alone in it either. As soon as Hannah's hope was reignited, she could begin to heal from her shame and pain while she waited to see God's promises fulfilled.

God's healing miracles in our lives aren't "if" situations; they are just a matter of timing—His timing. David here in this Psalm, like Hannah, is praising God for a miracle he hasn't seen happen yet. Why? Because he knows God hears him, and if he hears him he WILL act.

Cry out to God about the things in your heart that seem too broken to repair, too lost to restore, or too impossible to ever happen. Give Him space to work in the broken cracks of your heart. Even in your pain, disappointment, and waiting you can praise God because your hope is never misplaced when it's put in Him.

Look at the Pieces:

- Are there areas in your life where you feel like you're not enough? Have you taken those areas to God for healing and restoration or are you still sitting in shame trying to fix it yourself?

- What promise has God made you that you're still waiting for? Will you cling to hope or give up in the waiting?

- What's one way you can praise God in this season of waiting?

Prayer: *Jesus, I know in every space of my life where I feel like I'm not enough or like I'm missing something I'll never get back, your grace is there. I trust that the things in my life you haven't done yet are because of your favor on my life and a better plan you have in the future. It is not because you don't love me or because I've messed up your plans. Please give me peace and hope in the waiting. Allow my heart the freedom to praise you even before I see you moving. Thank you for the miracles you are bringing out of my pain.*

CHAPTER 3:
UNEXPECTED HEALING

John 5:1-18 [1]; Acts 3-4 [2]

Laying on the ground, staring up at everyone who passes by, in the same filth, same spot as yesterday and the thousands before it.

The paralytic man in John 5, is in a place many of us have been before. He's tired of trying and tired of hoping anything will change. The place where he's lying is a pool at Bethesda, which can either mean "house of grace" or "house of shame and disgrace" in Aramaic. It's kind of strange to me that it could mean two very opposite things, but I've learned God likes to work in that tension.

For those who stopped by, the people at the pool were issues, not names. They were just "the guy with one arm," "the lady with leprosy," "the man with an addiction," "the woman who was assaulted," "the single dad," "the woman with cancer..." the list goes on.

25

For thirty-eight years, this man was lying on the ground watching other people get into the pool and get healed. Every time he got a glimpse of what it would feel like to be whole and healed, only to realize again he couldn't reach it. That's soul crushing... hope crushing. It was easier at this point to settle for a normal he never wanted.

There was one man by the pool, and Jesus saw him. He wasn't the only one at the pool; there were multitudes. But Jesus saw *him*. And Jesus knew instinctively that he had been there a very long time. In fact, he'd been laying there longer than Jesus was on the earth.

Jesus spoke to him like a person, not a project. He wasn't saying, "I'm going to help the one who helps himself." He was looking for the one who *couldn't* help himself. The problem was he'd have to change the man's heart before he could fix his body.

Like the Shunammite woman, this man had given up hope of ever getting what he wanted most. Jesus asks him, "Do you want to be healed?" (v. 6). If you're someone who's still hoping that will happen, you just yell "Yes!" But this man was used to trying to help himself after thirty-eight years.

Even though Jesus asked if he wanted to *be* healed, the lame man started in with a list of reasons why he hadn't already healed himself. "I have no one." That's blame, abandonment, and loneliness talking. "Someone always beats me into the pool" (v.

7). That's trauma talking, telling him no matter what he tries it'll never be enough.

> So many of us abandon our hope for healing or wholeness and breakthrough because we're afraid of all the "what if's." We make peace with our brokenness.

Some of us sit in church week after week with the same issue and don't say yes to Jesus' healing. We once hoped Jesus would come through, and now it's excruciatingly painful to keep hoping for healing and breakthrough. So many of us abandon our hope for healing or wholeness and breakthrough because we're afraid of all the "what if's." We make peace with our brokenness. We'd rather say "It is what it is." or "I've just accepted this is my life." or "It's just the way I am."

If Jesus knew all of this about the lame man, why even bother asking if he wants to get well? As Steven Furtick, Pastor of Elevation Church, points out, "Before Jesus can help him walk, he has to help him want... [Because] repeated disappointment can become a sickness, and each time it comes around we have less hope that anything will change. So God has to deal with our desires."[3]

If this were a writing prompt in school, I imagine it would go something like, "Jesus walks up to a pool crowded with people who are sick and sees a paralyzed man who's been there thirty-eight years. What does he do next?"

I would probably go with one of three options for the plot of that story. In Option A, Jesus sits down on the mat next to the man and asks how he got there. He comforts him for a while and says, "I'll help you get into the pool next time the waters stir." In Option B, Jesus waves his hand over all the sick people at the pool and tells all of them they are healed. Then he walks away in a real "mic drop" kind of way. Option C casts Jesus as the tough coach, saying to the guy, "Really? After thirty-eight years you couldn't crawl an inch closer? Use your hands, and let's see if you can get to that pool! I'll drag your feet."

But as we know from the text, none of these scenes play out. Jesus asks the man if he wants to be healed because there is responsibility in healing. Healing means losing the victim mentality, letting go of the pain, and stepping away from the numbing.

He doesn't wave his hand over the ground like some magic trick because there is no intimacy or humanity in healing people in some mass public show. Jesus is a face to face, one on one, healer. And like Steven Furtick said, "Jesus has never taunted anyone into transformation."[4] Funny enough, Jesus doesn't even address the man's excuses. He just tells him, "Get up, take your bed, and walk" (v. 8).

As easy as that sounds to us, it must have taken some small amount of faith for him to try even one more time and risk disappointment or shame again.

Jesus is telling him to do three things he can't do: get up, take his mat, and walk. But he does it. And "at once the man is healed" (v. 9).

After all that time trying to fix it himself and failing, his healing comes when he simply gets up in faith. Faith is doing something Jesus has told you to do that you know you can't do without him.

When he stands up, his perspective changes, physically, and in every way. He is carrying the thing that once carried him, his mat, and it becomes a testament to Jesus' healing for him to tell others about. He starts walking because he can't stay where he's been now that he is free.

His healing wasn't a reward for his obedience. That would be religion. If just trying harder would have worked, he would have already been healed. The man, like many of us, didn't fail for lack of effort. But Jesus said, "Trust me." We can't let our trying get in the way of our trusting.

> **The blood of Jesus doesn't give you amnesia to forget the pain of the past, but it does give you a life beyond your past.**

After he's healed, Jesus finds the man in the synagogue, a place he wouldn't have been allowed while he was paralyzed. And he's there telling the crowd how Jesus healed him. Jesus ignores the disapproving looks of the religious who were just mad he'd healed on the Sabbath and instead he focuses on the heart of this man he healed. He tells him to "go and sin no more" (v. 14). Grace had fully covered him, but Jesus knew that living in darkness would lead him back to being on the mat spiritually.

We may be more comfortable sitting on the mat in our mess, but Jesus is in the transformation business. He wants to take our place of shame and turn it into a place of grace. If you're tired of trying to save relationships, tired of overcoming one thing after another, or tired of trying to fix yourself, then you're the one He's looking for.

Maybe you're the one this book was meant to reach. Be honest with Him about your skepticism and failed attempts to do this on your own. But then take one more step toward healing. Try one more time. Not in your own strength, but recognize that what Jesus did for you on the cross is bigger than what anyone or any circumstance has done to you. That'll be the day you get off the mat. The blood of Jesus doesn't give you amnesia to forget the pain of the past, but it does give you a life beyond your past.

卐卐卐

In Acts 3 we find another man who's paralyzed. But this man is done even asking for healing. He's just decided begging for money to get by is as good as it'll get for him.

Every day some people carry him to the gate outside the temple so he can beg for money from those going to worship. That's where John and Peter first meet him. The man asks Peter and John to put some coins in his jar, only hoping to get enough to feed himself today. But God had other plans.

Peter makes him look up at them, says they don't have any coins and then reaches out his hand. Then Peter, who's not known for being subtle, tells him, "In the name of Jesus Christ of Nazareth, rise up and walk!". As Peter takes him by the hand and pulls him up, "immediately his feet and ankles were made strong" (v. 6-7).

Time out! Neither Peter and John nor the paralyzed man were expecting a miracle. Sometimes we're so used to our pain and dysfunction, we're surprised God is good.

For over forty years, the man was paralyzed until one day he was miraculously healed. With God you're never too old and it's never too late for us to be healed and whole. This man's healing was four decades in the making, and yet, it was right on time.

Those areas in your life you've decided are forever paralyzed or broken, where you don't even have faith to ask for help any more, are the very places God wants to work His miraculous healing power in.

Healing can come unexpectedly and when we've given up. Healing can even start with someone else's faith for us. The beggar wouldn't have received his healing if he'd insisted on getting what he asked for. God was trying to give him something he'd long since given up on, but he had to decide if he was going to embrace the surprise or fight it.

It's harder to be surprised the older we get, and we usually like surprises less. Some of our biggest surprises may have been traumatic, so we're less surprisable and more cynical. That's the challenge of faith—not being more certain, but staying surprisable.

"Faith and nothing but faith put this man healed and whole right before your eyes" (v. 16).

When the man looked up at Peter and John, his tiny faith may have only allowed him to expect some coins, but it was enough faith for God to work with. I believe it was also, in part, Peter's faith that healed him. Your faith could help heal others who've settled for being broken and resigned to a life of being stuck *if* you can see past your own weakness.

Peter had a record of screwing things up, trying to help and only making things worse. God had to teach him not to be surprised anymore by his own weakness, but instead to be confident in God's strength. Most of us upon seeing the man begging, would have stopped at "I don't have any coins to give you." If God had given them a heads up that a man on their path would need money, they would have brought some change.

But their sympathy would have been an enablement that kept him on the mat. Enabling may feel kind, but it will never bring healing. Sometimes the most compassionate thing we can do for someone isn't to ask what they need in this moment, but to ask if they want healing. Once he was walking, he continued to hold onto Peter and John. God knows what healing we need, and he also knows what support we need in that healing.

The healed man began "walking and leaping and praising God" (v. 9). Notice none of the others at the temple who claimed to be worshipping God were doing that. Why not? Maybe they had been coming to God to change stuff without wanting Him to change them. Maybe they'd just stopped appreciating what God did for them and starting expecting it. Maybe they were afraid if he got off the mat, they'd lose their excuse for not changing.

Rich Wilkerson Jr., Pastor of VOUS Church, says, "The longer we wait for something, the more we lower our expectations."[5] If we raise our expectations to the level of our God's power, we won't be surprised by his favor and healing. In one text we see a man who thought he'd never be healed, and in the other, a man who wasn't ready to be healed. Neither had any hope until He arrived. But when hope arrived, they found healing wasn't far behind.

Look at the Pieces:

- If Jesus walked up to you face to face and asked what He could do for you, would you even bother asking for healing? What are your usual excuses or ways of avoiding being vulnerable with God?

- What you are surprised by says a lot about what you have assumed. What have you been surprised by lately? What does this indicate about your assumptions of God? Of yourself?

- Is there someone in your life who is stuck that God is asking you to reach out a hand to? Are your attempts to help them enabling or healing?

Prayer: *Jesus, you know the parts of my heart that are laying on the mat, paralyzed and stuck. You want to heal me, and I pray that you give me the faith to believe healing is happening now. It doesn't matter how long I've been in this spot. What matters is that "all things hold together in you" (Col. 1:17), including my broken heart and life. You have made me "more than a conqueror" (Rom. 8:37), so if I take Your hand and stand up, nothing can stop me from walking in wholeness. Please tear down the lies I've believed that try to keep me on the mat. Help me learn to walk again so that I can reach out a hand in the future to help someone else get off their mat. Thank you for seeing and helping the one, thank you for healing ME.*

Chapter 4:
When Hope Seems Adrift

Exodus 2 & 3 [1]; Numbers 32 [2]

All Moses' mother wanted was a family, not a Pharaoh who wanted every boy in Egypt killed.

Moses was born into a painful and traumatic situation. I can't imagine the feelings of helplessness, fear, and guilt that mother must have experienced. Like so many moms in tough circumstances, she didn't want to leave her child or lose him. But she had very few choices. It was risk him being discovered and killed or try to hide him.

She wrapped him up as carefully as she could, quieted him to sleep, and placed him in a sealed basket.

> ...if God writes our story He can turn our loss into a miracle.

When she thought no one in her master's house was watching, she slipped down to the river and set the basket in it. I imagine tears slipped down her face as she turned her back to walk away. She had to hope someone else would step up and protect him or somehow God would hide him.

As she went back to work, there's no way her mind was on anything other than him. Then something happened she probably never anticipated. Pharaoh's daughter, who'd found Moses in the river, sent her a request to come be the child's nurse. Not only had Moses been spared from death, but Pharaoh's daughter had taken him in as her own.

That had to be the last place his mom would have expected or wanted him-in the house of the man trying to murder him. But God was writing this story. His mother was reunited with him as his nurse for the first few years of his life. At some point she wasn't needed as a nurse anymore and had to give him up again, but by then he was safe and alive.

We give Moses' mom lots of credit because of how God worked the story out. But truth be told, she could have just been acting in fear, and probably was to some extent. She felt inadequate to protect her child, and yet God worked. She experienced a heavy loss having to give up being his mother, and yet God worked. God provided for Moses even when his mother couldn't.

Moses' mother was willing to let him go and trust God, and God worked miracles because of it. God can do that in our lives with the people or things we're willing to leave in His hands. It may not be in the same way, but if God writes our story He can turn our loss into a miracle.

So many of us know the pain of a mom passing away, leaving children behind or someone having to walk away from children they loved for a number of reasons. It's almost unbearable. It takes faith to let go and trust God to protect them and guide them no matter what. But letting go of someone you can no longer protect isn't the end of hope. Sometimes it's the biggest act of hope. Hope they'll get help you can't give them. Hope they'll be safe in God's hands. Hope that God's ways are higher than your own.

Because Moses' mother had to give him up, doors were opened for him in Pharaoh's household that never would have otherwise. But it wasn't without it's trauma for both Moses and his mother.

Moses was resilient. However, resilience didn't erase the reality of the childhood trauma he'd experienced. God would have to heal him from that. Growing up at Pharaoh's house didn't just mean fancy clothes and school classes, it meant imperialism and racial tension.

After all, Moses' name means "drawn out." He didn't think he fit anywhere. He didn't fit with Egyptians or Hebrews. It meant Moses struggled with abandonment issues and a lack of identity. We can see in his adult years how these struggles have shaped him.

That pain rears its head up when he sees an Egyptian beating a Hebrew, and Moses kills the Egyptian slave driver. After being spared from death himself as a child, here he is, now a murderer. He doesn't know how to deal with the shame and the threats of being exposed, and he runs into the wilderness.

For forty years, Moses grew up in tension. Then the next forty years he spends hiding in Midian. He went from being the guy confident enough to strike an Egyptian out of a sense of justice, to a guy hiding in the desert that doesn't even trust his ability to speak in public. How does that happen?

Shame. Shame will make you do all kinds of things outside your normal character. Ronnie Johnson of Red Rocks Church says, "Shame is your soul trying to punish you for something God already paid for."[3] For forty years, while Moses started a family in a foreign place and hid out in the desert, he was beating himself up over that murder and ruining things for himself. That feeling of failure only made him retreat more and tell himself he was just going to make it on his own.

One day while Moses was out tending flocks in the field alone, God showed up. He put on quite a show by setting a bush on fire without letting it burn, and it definitely got Moses' attention. God tells him the suffering of His people hasn't gone unnoticed, and He is sending Moses to Pharaoh to bring them out of Egypt. Moses immediately questions his identity, and asks, "Who am I...?" (v. 3:11).

All he knew himself to be is the guy who tried to help and ended up a murderer and failure. God didn't focus on who Moses is, he told him who HE is—The Great I AM.

Judah Smith, Pastor of Churchome, brilliantly states, "God doesn't make us better versions of ourselves. We don't need improvement; we need saving. We live in a culture that tells us we are the problem but we're also the solution. That math doesn't add up! Our hope is not in our fear, our failures, or even our faithfulness. Jesus is better than all of this. He is our only hope."[4] Notice, God doesn't go get stuff Moses would need for the mission. He *is* what Moses needs.

Hebrews 3 describes Moses as a model of faithfulness and says he "was faithful in all God's house as a servant". Really? He doesn't seem like a model citizen or bastion of faith to me. Moses was afraid. He ran. He was content to avoid his purpose. He wasn't ready to be obedient even after a burning bush. He made excuses about needing Aaron to speak for him, even though he was very well educated. He had an anger problem all throughout his time as leader of the Israelites.

But I think that's the whole point of Moses' story. God's calling of Moses exposed his deepest level of insecurity. Moses told God there was no way he could do it. And that's *why* God chose him. He knew Moses wouldn't try to do it alone.

This story isn't about Moses being perfect or courageous. It's about God taking our doubtfulness and fear-filled lives and turning them into lives full of faith. He turned Moses into someone he never thought he could be. Maybe there was a part of Moses that thought he'd been spared for a purpose, but I doubt he ever envisioned this grand plan.

> God can bring us back home far more quickly than it takes us to run away.

He'd been drawn out in the midst of Pharaoh's bloodshed because God had a purpose for him, but it would take him eighty years to start acting as a man of faith.

If you drive around town on local roads, stopping at all the lights, and going into stores along the way, it can take you over an hour to cross Denver, the city where I live. However, when you get tired of driving around and decide it's time to come home, you can make it in twenty to thirty minutes on the highway (assuming there's no massive construction)!

It's like that with God. It took Moses forty years to wander around the desert and set up a life he was just settling for. It only took him a few days to come back to Egypt with God's guiding hand.

God can bring us back home far more quickly than it takes us to run away. We may be tempted to conclude that we're not getting anywhere because there's something wrong with us. News flash! There's something wrong with ALL of us. That's why we need transformation, not improvement. We need to walk close to the burning bush—what God's trying to show us—and let Him start working in us.

The delay wasn't because God was debating whether he was the guy for the job. It was because God needed to heal Moses from some of those tendencies his trauma had created. There are pieces of those we lose in our lives that get lodged in us and become a part of us. We carry them with us and their stories live on in our hearts. For Moses, that meant carrying the promises his mom had spoken over him about being used by God to save his people, but it also meant carrying the weight of not having her in his life.

He was used to avoiding and stonewalling the tough things, maybe out of self-defense or maybe even to hurt the people he thought had failed him. He wanted to isolate himself to get away from it all, but that didn't offer true rest because he couldn't avoid the battle inside himself.

His default was stressing and striving to take things into his own hands. That's what we do when we're desperate and hurting. Every time he took things into his hands and failed, he believed the enemy's lies more and more. Eventually he just surrendered to them. He believed the lie that his past had ruined whatever plan God may have originally had for him.

Even when we dwell on it, God chooses not to remember our sins (Heb. 8:12). When we're burning down whatever and whoever is around us out of pain, fear, or shame, He ignites a different kind of fire inside us. It doesn't consume anything around us, but instead ignites a healing process within us. God turns the places we're avoiding into places of His anointing.[5]

卐卐卐

Moses' most well known years come from the period of Israel's exodus from Egypt. The ten plagues, crossing the Red Sea, and following God into the desert are just the highlight reel. But even though that part of the story reads like a superhero comic, Moses' journey of healing was still very much unfinished.

Trauma is like an alarm going off inside us that we can't turn off with the flip of a switch.. We ignore it but sometimes that drives us crazy. Sometimes we get used to it, but that has its own consequences too. Moses tried both, but we saw his anger rise up when he killed the Egyptian. That same unresolved anger still pops up for Moses with the people of Israel in the desert.

When his heart is in pain or he puts all the pressure of leading the Israelites on his own shoulders, he does things like strike rocks he's supposed to speak to and throw tablets God gave him for instruction. He gets scared of failing or angry about what he can't control, and that pain lashes out in ways that hurt him and those around him.

Shortly before Moses' death, Israel camped out on the opposite side of the Jordan River from the Promised Land and some of them just wanted to permanently stay there. They were tired of fighting. Earlier in his life Moses' trauma would have told him to settle when he got close to his dreams because it was easier to settle than risk being disappointed or ashamed. But this time is different. He gives clear directions to Joshua, his successor, and all the people that they will "live long in the land [they] are going *over* the Jordan to possess" (Deut. 32:47,ESV). They are going to the other side, not settling because they were scared.

> We may feel like we've missed our chance or burned it all to the ground, but God is a builder, a repairer, and a restorer.

Anything God promises us requires a fight. Even if you think you don't want what God promises, you will still have to fight in this life anyway. So why settle? Why not fight for God's best for you instead of just fighting against the enemy? Settling is fine if the only person you're accountable to is yourself, but you're not! So fight for your healing. Fight for your relationships. Fight for the future God has prepared for you.

Moses' disobedience to God at points along the way meant he'd only get to see the Promised Land from a distance, but not enter it. However, it's clear God healed his heart from his childhood wounds and made him whole. There's no other way he could have been so confident in the future, after all he'd been through.

He learned to be content, grateful for all God *had* done even if He didn't do anything more. He wasn't complacent. He experienced God's rescue more than once. He saw God pull off impossible victories. He felt God's loving pursuit when he was hiding in shame. And he felt God heal him and use him to help others.

We may feel like we've missed our chance or burned it all to the ground, but God is a builder, a repairer, and a restorer. The first eighty years of Moses' 120-year long life weren't wasted. They may have been full of fear, selfishness, avoidance, and even violence, YET God redeemed his life. Even when we think it's all lost, God isn't done.

Striving for what we've lost won't work, but God will meet us where we are and show us hope that's still ahead. Failure isn't the end of hope, but the beginning of God's hand at work. When He restores our hope, He can begin to heal us from our loss and our failures.

<u>Look at the Pieces:</u>

- Are there areas of trauma or loss that you are running from all the while carrying them with you?

- What steps can you take to let God start healing those wounds so you can walk in victory and wholeness?

- What lies about your past or yourself have you believed to be bigger than God's plan for you? (Consider writing them down today and finding scriptures that declare who God says you are instead.)

<u>Prayer:</u> *Jesus, I have failed. I have past mistakes I would rather run from than face. I've believed lies about myself that have kept me in hiding. But no more! I don't have to be enough and never will be. You are my hope and sufficiency. When I am tempted to settle based on what my eyes can see, help me to see with eyes of faith. No matter what the path to my healing looks like, help me trust You and hold onto You, my victorious hope (Heb. 3:6). Write my story of redemption and restoration as only You can.*

CHAPTER 5:

THE TENSION OF HOPE

1 Kings 18-19 [1]

"After a long time, in the third year, the word of the Lord came to Elijah" (18:1). Three years prior to this text Elijah took a massive risk and walked in to tell the king there would be no rain for the next three years. Since then, he's been hiding in the desert where God sent him ravens to bring him breakfast. How crazy is that?

Part of me thinks it would have been so cool to see that magic trick every morning, but it also sounds kind of disgusting! I can't imagine how lonely it must have been to have spent 1,095 days in the desert by yourself.

It's finally time for the rain to come, but God doesn't instantly fix the drought. Elijah still has to act. He has to go see the king—a king who probably wouldn't be happy to see him.

King Ahab hasn't been able to find Elijah for the last three years, but when God decides it's time, he makes their paths cross. Ahab and his household manager, Obadiah, are out in the fields scouring the land for a little grass to get by. In the meantime, God is sending them the real answer to their prayers in the form of someone they didn't want to hear—Elijah.

Elijah's welcome from the king is as brisk as he anticipated...awkward! But he doesn't back down. God sent him to bring the healing rain, and he isn't going to be stopped by the kings' reign. (You know you like that pun!)

I teach middle school, so I see this going down like a hallway chest-puffing match. The king calls Elijah "the troubler of Israel" (v. 17), and Elijah just throws shade right back. Elijah blames the king for Israel's troubles and says, "grab 850 prophets of your gods and meet me at Mount Carmel at 3:00" (v.18-19, *paraphrased*).

The king rallies all his people and prophets to Mount Carmel for a showdown. Elijah lays down the ground rules. The first god to bring fire on the altar will be the one true God. While Ahab's prophets cry out to Baal dramatically and violently, Elijah just talks smack.

Then, when it's his turn, Elijah starts by repairing the altar of God that was torn down. He starts showing off a little and digs a trench around the altar. He pours water over the altar and the wood three times until everything is soaked and it fills the trench. Good luck getting wet wood to light! But he prays, "Answer me, O Lord, answer me, that these people may know that you, O Lord, are God, and that you have turned their hearts back" (v. 37).

Elijah's prayer is clear: he expects the Lord to show up so the people can physically see His power and turn their hearts back to Him. And that's exactly what He does. God brings the fire to consume the altar, and the people turn against the prophets of Baal, proclaiming "The Lord—He is God!" (v. 39).

> Sometimes hoping feels a lot like waiting.

So far everything has gone according to plan, and Elijah tells King Ahab to go down off the mountain and start partying because the rain is coming. The king's ego is bruised from his loss on Mount Carmel, but he's hoping to focus attention on the positive-the end of the drought. Meanwhile, Elijah isn't ready to join the party yet. Instead, he climbs the mountain and puts his head between his knees to wait.

Maybe he is praying or maybe he was just resting from a long, hot day. He sends his servant to look for a cloud seven times before anything happens. (I would've hated being that guy!) The seventh time he goes out, the servant tells Elijah he sees a tiny cloud the size of a man's hand. Elijah proclaims a heavy rain is coming and sends word to the king. *Then* he takes off running himself!

Sometimes hoping feels a lot like waiting. It seems like a long time before God answers that prayer you've been waiting for. But God doesn't waste the waiting. While Elijah waits for rain to come, he ends up raising a widow's son to life (Exodus 17), like Elisha would later do for the Shunammite woman. And even though that was miraculous and God used him, it didn't mean the waiting was any less difficult.

Sometimes it's not the big showy prayers that require the most faith, but those we whisper alone, over and over, while we wait. Prayers that require us to keep going back to God to see if he's doing anything yet. Those prayers in the waiting require a faith that won't let go.

God's miracles of restoration require us to risk our comfort to be obedient to God. It may feel risky to reach out to someone you've hurt, get help from a counselor, or open up to a friend about what's really going on. But without that risk, you'll stay in the lonely, desert place, wondering when the drought will come instead of asking for rain.

🔯🔯🔯

After the miracle of fire on Mount Carmel, the people return to worshipping God, but not everyone's heart has changed. Jezebel, King Ahab's wife, hears the news and decides to push things right over the edge. Picture Cruella Deville with her most evil laugh.

She sends a letter to Elijah that says, in so many words, "I'm going to kill you". Maybe her ego and security is feeling threatened, thinking Elijah gained too much power. Maybe she is ashamed that her god Baal has been royally trampled. Maybe she is mad that she lost the profits she had been making from the people as they sacrificed to Baal. Regardless, her threats are enough to scare Elijah and send him running.

> He *believes* he's alone, so he makes sure he is alone. He *feels* like he's abandoned, so he abandons his servant.

That was a quick change of heart from the big mouthed guy who was calling down fire on Mount Carmel just the other day. Why?

Maybe that little fear he had that God wouldn't come through came rushing back with the threats of one woman. He'd overcome it with his own faith until now, but now he feared God wouldn't really come through 100% of the way. Maybe he feared God had come through only to disappear again. Maybe the rain would only be a sprinkle and not end the drought. Maybe he was disappointed the whole kingdom didn't turn to God, like he hoped. Perhaps he was angry or exhausted. Maybe he was just human, and his fear became bigger than his faith in that moment.

Regardless, he goes with one of the typical human fear responses, he RUNS.

He also pulls another fear move and leaves his servant so he can be alone. He *believes* he's alone, so he makes sure he is alone. He *feels* like he's abandoned, so he abandons his servant.

Elijah runs because that seems easier than facing his fear or resting in his faith. But if God lets him retreat, Jezebel would hunt him down and Elijah would die. We've all had "I've had enough" moments, and it's okay to throw our hands up to God in those moments. But instead, Elijah does what we often try to; he attempts to take everything on himself. He says, "I have had enough, Lord. Take my life; I'm no better than my ancestors" (v. 4).

Not only are his ancestors irrelevant here, but it's not about HIM. It never was. It was God who showed up at Mount Carmel and God who brought the rain, not Elijah. But somewhere between his run to Jezreel in the rain and his run to the tree in the desert, he's decided it's all on him.

There is a medical condition called "tension pneumothorax". It occurs when air builds up in our chest cavity, pressing on the lungs and heart. Pain and fear work like that. They weigh on us internally, and pressure builds up until we can't breathe. They lead us to give up because we'll never *be* enough. We have to release that pressure because God is the only one who will ever be enough.

God doesn't scold Elijah while he is in his panicked mental and emotional state. He just sends an angel, like the first UberEats delivery driver. The angel wakes Elijah up and tells him to get up and eat something. Next to him is the pinnacle of comfort foods—carbs. A second time the angel comes back and says, "Get up and eat, for the journey is too much for you" (v. 7).

When he was running from fear into the desert he only made it a day, but now that he's strengthened by God, he makes it a 40-day journey. However, even though Elijah has gotten up from under the tree and decided he's not going to give up, he still feels alone and hopeless.

Instead of going back to face the music or going to a friend's house to ride it out, he climbs into a cave. When God asks him, "What are you doing here?" he tells God, "I am the only one [of the prophets] left, and now they are trying to kill me" (v. 9-10). In short, "I'm alone, and there's no way out."

That's when God reveals himself to Elijah again. God tells him to go to the mouth of the cave because He's about to pass by. But God isn't in the earthquake, wind, or fire that comes by. (All I can think about is the band name every time I read that story!) Instead, He comes to Elijah in a gentle whisper.

That means Elijah has to get quiet to hear God's voice. When he does, God tells him to go back to the place he felt God had failed him, the place of his fear, because his purpose there isn't done. He is to anoint new kings and new prophets to succeed him.

Elijah finds and anoints Elisha as the next prophet. If he had not obeyed God in his darkest season, there would have been no prophet Elisha. No prophet Elisha to raise the Shunammite woman's son or fill the widow's jars with oil.

Sometimes God's way of moving us forward is leading us back to the places and seasons where we feel He failed us so that He can show us how it's really supposed to end. When we go back to face those fears, we can expect to watch God work in us. Our obedience, even in the dark, plants seeds that will grow long after our seasons of pain are over. But if we refuse to be obedient, it won't just have an impact on us. It will affect future generations.

You can't have fear without faith. It's just faith put toward imagining a negative future. In Elijah's case, when he was afraid, he ran for his life, but he also ran *from* the life God had for him.

Erwin McManus, Pastor of Mosaic, says, "When you run from your fears, you're running from God because God is never running from your fears. God doesn't go anywhere when we run from our fears. He is waiting for us to come back and face them because our future and freedom is on the other side of that fear."[2] Don't waste your life running. Turn and fight *for* your life.

When we are depressed or fearful, we tend to manifest our deepest fears like Elijah did by pushing his servant away and walking alone into the desert. But even when we're ready to give up, God is ready to get us up and going again.

He knows even the menial things we need when we're hurting, like food and rest. He's not above providing them for us, and He's patient enough to stay beside us while we recover. He doesn't

> **No one can fight the battle within you except you and God.**

condemn us when we're weak or shame us for not being able to get up on our own. He cares for us and heals us, just like he did for Elijah.

God knew Elijah was not ready yet, but He wasn't done with him either. There was a battle within Elijah that God had to help him overcome before he was ready to face those fears and heal. Sometimes we're weary because we're fighting a battle we weren't meant to fight alone. No one can fight the battle within you except you and God.

Sometimes we're tired of bouncing between hopeful and hopeless when it comes to our healing or the healing of others. As my friend Kate says, "Sometimes we're stuck between the past we don't want to revisit and the future we're afraid we won't find."

When we feel hopeless and lost, that's when we're ready to come close and hear God's voice. Only He can be our surgeon and our friend at the same time. He will meet us in our darkest, loneliest places to heal us from our fear and failures. When we embrace the tension of hope that lies between "God is working" and "I can't fix myself," we'll see Him work a miracle.

Look at the Pieces:

- There may be people in our lives who, like Jezebel, don't handle our healing well and threaten the progress God is making in us. Do the people in your life want to keep you in your past or do they accept your present and want all God has for you in your future?

- Is God whispering to you today, "why are you here?" Are you staying in a place or season you aren't meant to be in? Are you staying in the cave alone?

- What fears have you run from that you need to go back and face in order to walk forward in healing?

Prayer: *God, I need you to show up for me in big, bold ways, like you did on Mount Carmel. But more than anything I pray You will show up for me in the dark, lonely places. Help me to press into You when I'm scared and feel alone so that I can hear the whisper of Your voice. Give me courage to face the fears I'm running from so I can walk in freedom instead of hiding. When I'm at the end of my rope and want to give up, I know You will comfort my soul. Thank You for not leaving me to fight this battle alone. You don't give up on me because my purpose is so much bigger than just surviving. Give me hope for the future You have in store for me.*

GLUE THAT HEALS

In kintsugi pottery the lacquer or glue that is used is extremely precious. Extracting just one cup of the needed sap from a tree will cost the tree its life.1 It is an astounding sacrifice, but a necessary one for restoration.

The same sacrifice is needed for our healing. God's love poured out for us on the cross is the glue that binds our broken pieces back together. Without it, we will never be whole.

His gracious hands work tediously on our hearts one day at a time. Completing just one kintsugi restoration can take up to three months.2 It's not something the Potter will rush.

As you dive into the lives we see in this section, let the love of God start to glue you back together. Let Him heal your broken soul.

It will require patient work, one crack at a time. And it will reveal your imperfections. But if you'll allow God to heal the breakage, your scars will become places of beauty and strength.

CHAPTER 6:

HELP TO HEAL

2 Samuel 21:1-22 [1]

As a middle school teacher, I am perpetually trying to solve problems I didn't create. Drama between students, rough home lives, poor educational practices... the list goes on and on. We all have problems we inherit that aren't our fault.

In 2 Samuel 21, David inherits something really dysfunctional that isn't his fault. The chapter starts with him cleaning up the mess caused by the former king, and man who tried to kill him, Saul! There is a famine because Saul disobeyed God and killed the Gibeonites.

David is left to try and rectify the relationship with the Gibeonites so the famine can end for all the Israelites. However, David's biggest obstacle isn't overcoming problems caused by Saul, but overcoming his own stubborn, survival, isolation instincts.

By this point David had been chased by Saul for years, fought many battles and had many victories, had a family, acquired lots of wealth, and became very renowned. He certainly wasn't lazy, careless, weak, old, or unprepared. He was a good man and a good king, who was only trying to be responsible and take care of those he was supposed to protect.

In his first attempt to reconcile with the Gibeonites, he hands over some of Saul's descendants to be killed. He buries the bones of Saul, Jonathan, and their descendants, and thinks he's solved the problem. Then he turns around and "once again there was a battle" (v. 15). This war isn't a new one either.

The Philistines, descendants of Goliath, are back for more. David has changed since the days of killing Goliath with a slingshot, but some things inside him are still the same. He was seventeen when he killed Goliath; now he's forty and fighting the same enemy. Only now the stakes are higher because people are counting on him as king.

In true heroic style, David goes down with his men to fight the Philistines, but fights to the point of exhaustion. We can be anointed and still find ourselves exhausted at the same time.[2] The same passion and strength that made David successful previously are exhausting him this time.

While he's trying to rally and stay in the fight a soldier from the opposing army, named Ishbi-Benob ("Ish" for short) brandishes a 7-pound sword and yells, "I'm going to kill you David!" Back in the day, Goliath had a 15-pound sword, and this guy only has a 7-pound sword. So why can't David defeat him? Because he's exhausted.

David is a lot like the lion he killed while he was a shepherd. He is used to protecting everyone else, used to working through the pain and trying not to let anyone see him sweat. David was made strong to survive things like bear attacks, but the same strength put him into survival mode later in life. He starts to look more and more like the wounded lion in this poem.

Can you tell me the behavior of a Wounded Lion? Have you studied him? Do you know what to expect, when you can't see his injury?

I once knew of a Wounded Lion, his behavior was very odd. I watched him from outside his habitat. He carried on, leading his kind long after he was hurt. The other lions could not see he was injured. He never let on that he had a weakness. Though he felt defeated. He had scars from many battles on the outside. The Wounded Lion stood strong.

When the pain was more than he could bear he would roar to make known to the pride he was still OK. After all it was his job to protect his "Pride". Then he would retreat to the darkest cave he could find, as far away from the light as he could go. And there in the isolation he would lick his wounds. He would try to rest. But there was no rest for the lion because he knew he had to get up again and go back to being in charge.

There in his solitary confinement he would replay the battle that brought him down this time. He questioned his own decisions. He doubted his own strength. He looked within himself and came back without answers.

As I watched the Wounded Lion, I desperately wanted to help. I wanted to go with him to the darkest places. But he insisted by his stature that he go alone. I knew that if I got too close to the wounded lion he would hurt me. Out of instinct, he could destroy me in an effort to protect himself. So I kept my distance. And I watched. I loved him. I somehow could feel his pain. I studied his highs and lows. I noticed he had good days and bad. I watched as his eating behaviors would change. And somehow he continues to roar. His beautiful mane still reflected the sunlight from the mountain tops. His walk was still steadfast as the King. His stroll, still with purpose.

As he looked at his great kingdom, he admired the lioness, all of them. I could tell in his eyes he wondered why they stayed. He looked at his offspring with great pride and hoped that one day they would know how valuable he was to his kind.

I wondered how long would the Wounded Lion take to heal? Would he die in the darkness? Would he disappear and never return? Would he become a prey to the enemy?

Only time would tell how the Wounded Lion would survive. I wondered if I would be around to see him overcome what was meant to take him out.[3]

Sylina Mumpower LiBasci

Anytime we're exhausted, the battle gets harder to fight. He needs a new strategy. His solo sling shot worked okay back then, but going it alone now is about to get him killed. When you face something that scares you, you don't always rise to new levels. You usually sink back to the same level. As Steven Furtick says, "You go back inside yourself and keep counsel with the most unreliable source-you unchecked."[4]

We all get weary and need help. We are only "treasures in jars of clay" (2 Cor. 4:7). We're human. What stinks is when we get tired over battles we don't have to fight, we fight internal battles alongside the external ones. When you're defensive and no one is attacking you, you're fighting an internal battle. If you don't recognize the fear or insecurity or pain as the same battle you've fought before, you'll exhaust yourself fighting it over and over instead of conquering it.

> ## Anytime we're exhausted, the battle gets harder to fight.

Like us, David can't use the same tactics he did in the past. He has to grow into the current season. If he keeps fighting like he did when he had no help, he is going to die.

But God didn't expect David, as strong as he was, to fight alone. So he sent Abishai.

🔳🔳🔳

David is exhausted and probably not sure he'll make it out of this battle alive, "but Abishai… came to David's rescue" (v. 17). Abishai is David's nephew, a leader in his army, and has been in other battles with David. His name even means "father of a gift."

We don't know much else about Abishai. It doesn't say he was a stronger warrior, a better person, or owed David anything. He just showed up, as God's gift to David. This wasn't the first time God sent someone to help David fight or to save his life. When Saul was trying to kill him, Jonathan helped him escape. If he hadn't accepted Jonathan's help or trusted him then, he probably wouldn't ever have been king.

In this battle, if he's threatened by Abishai thinking he isn't really here to help him or he's prideful and says he doesn't need help, it's over. David will likely be killed while Abishai looks on helplessly.

> In survival mode you go back to stuff you left in the dark.

Thankfully, that's not what happens. Abishai strikes the Philistine down and kills him. "Then David's men swore to him, saying, 'Never again will you go out with us to battle, so that the lamp of Israel will not be extinguished" (v. 17). David's men were protective of the other light: David. He was too important and had too big of a purpose to keep taking on the brunt of the battle himself.

If we don't upgrade how we fight our battles, our light will go out too. In survival mode you go back to stuff you left in the dark. The unhealthy habits, the untrue thoughts, the unhelpful people. But you don't need to do that anymore. You have Abishai. God has given you help in the form of people, but he's also given all of us Jesus to stand between us and the darkness, the depression, and the attack.

When we're tired, out of ideas, and done with people, we want God to send us an angel to rescue us from the situation. But God didn't send an angel to rescue David. He sent a person. Steven Furtick says, "When God sends you someone who sees potential that you can't see past your pain, hold onto them. When they have nothing to gain by loving you but love you anyway, don't let them go."[5]

We must keep our enemies at a distance and our Abishai's close. Instead, we spend our time stirring up imaginary battles in our souls and replaying lies in our head instead of keeping focused on the truth and the love of those in our life. If we push away the Abishai God sends us, we'll die at the hands of Ish while pushing away the gift of the Father.

After the battle where Abishai rescued David, there were still more enemies that came to fight. They are described vividly in v.19-21. I wonder if David hadn't taken Abishai's help, would he have been around to see those other victories? Between "once again there was a battle" in verse 15 and "never again," in verse 17 it wasn't about the enemy he faced; it was about the decisions he made.

Our internal issues and generational struggles will come back around to us. That's a given. The question is, will we learn to lean into the help God sends? Or will we try to keep fighting on our own? Healing is a process that always requires help. God never meant for us to fight alone, so when he sends us help, don't push it away.

Get the Glue:

- Is there something dysfunctional in your life that you inherited and you need to address to open your heart up to healing?

- Are there areas of your life where you're being defeated because you're drained?

- Are you pushing away an Abishai God is sending to help you?

Prayer: *Jesus, please show me the Abishais in my life. Give me the humility to accept help in my battles and the confidence to believe I am not in this alone. Help my heart to repent and consider where I've fallen. Show me where I've brought my enemies too close and pushed my Abishai away. Guard my light: my passion, perspective, and purpose. Open doors to reestablish things I've lost and reinvent things I've failed at. Thank You for always being my Abishai, even when I push away Your help. As I grow and heal, show me who I can be an Abishai for. Don't let my stubborn strength or survival mode tendencies get in the way of my healing.*

CHAPTER 7:
DEAD TO RIGHT
Luke 8:39-56 [1]

When you think about athletes like LeBron James, Tom Brady, Serena Williams, and so many more you automatically expect greatness every time they play their respective sports. I have zero athletic abilities, and yet when I go to a sporting event or watch one on TV that I'm passionate about, I expect the team or person I'm yelling at to perform at the highest level. It's hypocritical maybe, but those are just my expectations.

Jesus starts off this chapter in Luke 8 setting the bar real high! He calms a storm with his words and heals a demon-possessed man. He tells the man he heals to "return home and tell how much God has done for you" (v. 39). And that's exactly what the man does. So when Jesus comes back to that place, there is a crowd expecting to see him. They don't come to cheer; they come with expectations about what they want Jesus to do for them.

> ... his desperation for healing makes him humble enough to fall at Jesus' feet.

Jairus is one of those waiting with expectation. When he sees Jesus, he falls at his feet and pleads with Jesus to come to his house because his only daughter, who is just twelve, is dying. Jairus could pull the "power card" as a synagogue ruler and demand Jesus come with him, but his desperation for healing makes him humble enough to fall at Jesus' feet. He is about to lose his only child. It doesn't get more desperate than that.

Jesus is apparently swayed by Jairus and starts to head to his house with the crowds pushing in around him. That's when he's interrupted...

A woman is in the crowd who's been fighting a shameful and debilitating bleeding issue for twelve years. She doesn't think she's worthy to even speak to Jesus or ask him to heal her. She's already asked every doctor and tried everything she can to fix it, "but no one could heal her" (v. 43).

She squeezes through the crowd, risking being crushed herself, being stoned to death for getting too close as an "unclean" person (by religious laws)[2], and being disappointed one more time. It's all on the line, but she reaches out anyway, touching Jesus' robe from behind, probably hoping no one would notice.

"Immediately her bleeding stopped" (v.44). She notices at the same time Jesus does.

Jesus says, "Someone touched me; I know that power has gone out from me. Then the woman, seeing that she could not go unnoticed, came trembling and fell at his feet. In the presence of all the people, she told why she touched him and how she had been instantly healed" (v. 46-47). Exposure in the healing process is scary and vulnerable, even if we're revealing our brokenness to God who already knows it all.

She has to come clean about her issue to the crowd in order to declare how Jesus healed her. Our healing story is meant to be shared with others for God's glory and their healing, but that will come at a risk to us too.

Jesus says to the woman, "Daughter, your faith has healed you. Go in peace" (v. 48). He calls her "daughter," something she likely hasn't been called in a long time. In that day someone deemed "unclean" wouldn't have been allowed to live with their family. She would have been ostracized, on the outskirts of town.

Jesus, in an instant, doesn't just heal her body, but heals the loneliness she's been feeling for so long. Jesus could have condemned her to be stoned, according to the law, but he doesn't. Nor does he tell her she should have had enough faith to ask him for healing face-to-face and he doesn't ask her for anything in return. He affirms the small faith she has and tells her to go in peace.

Everyone in the crowd was waiting for Jesus, but the one person who thought she was unworthy to ask for His help is the one he chooses to heal. Jesus doesn't see us as unworthy, but we do have to get humble and desperate for our healing or someone else's. It's not because Jesus likes to see us hurting. It's because He knows we have to get to the end of what we can do before our pride moves out of the way and we can let healing in.

When we feel like we've tried and failed over and over to heal ourselves, we sometimes feel like we don't have the right to ask God for help anymore. We certainly don't want anyone to see us reach out again because what if it doesn't work this time either?

The woman here had tried everything and everyone to get healing, but kept coming up short. It's no wonder she was trying to hide in the crowd. We often try to hide our deepest hurts and broken pieces, and the longer they go unhealed the more we try to hide them.

She only had enough courage to slip up behind Jesus and reach for the edge of his robe, and yet that was enough to heal her. If all you've got left is a little bit of courage and a little bit of faith, reach out anyway. That's all it takes if you're reaching out to Jesus. She gave everything to other physicians to heal her and got nothing, but she reached out once to Jesus and was healed.

Jesus gave her the faith she needed to be made well, because faith is not from us. But she had to believe He could do it for *her* in order for His power to be released. When she was willing to get close to Jesus, His power went out to heal her. He no longer walks the earth in bodily form, but the person of the Holy Spirit is always near us. We just have to have an ounce of faith to reach out. That's when the power of God can work miracles in our lives.

卐卐卐

In the meantime, as Jairus watches this beautiful miracle from the sidelines, I wonder how his faith is doing. If I'm Jairus, I'm thinking, "Come on! You can come back to this woman later. She's dealt with this for twelve years; she'll last another few hours. My daughter can't wait! I've already been waiting for you to get here. I can't keep waiting!"

But it doesn't say that Jairus tried to hurry Jesus. That's a sign of his faith all by itself. While Jesus was speaking to the woman, someone in Jairus' household comes and tells Jairus his greatest fear has come true. His daughter is dead, and he shouldn't bother Jesus anymore.

Scripture doesn't describe how Jairus responds, but any loving father I know would've lost it. There would have been tears and grief expressed through anger as he yelled, "Why did you let this happen?" Maybe even a total collapse on the ground.

But Jesus doesn't even leave time for any of that. He hears the news Jairus is told, and turns to say, "Don't be afraid; just believe and she will be healed" (v. 50). Again, if I'm that dad, I'm thinking, "She WILL BE healed? That ship has sailed. We're too late because you slowed down for that other lady back there. How are you going to heal someone who's already dead?" Maybe he was thinking some of those things, but he had enough to try, because he takes Jesus to his house anyway.

> When we think all hope is lost or that a relationship or situation is dead, we need to bring Jesus into the room anyway.

When Jesus arrives at Jairus' house, he finds a house full of weeping and mourning. It doesn't sound like they are hopeful that the girl is going to be healed. In fact, when he tells them to stop crying because she's not really dead. They just laugh. No one believes him.

They think they know more with their logical human minds about the situation than Jesus does. And *yet* Jesus works a miracle because this father had enough faith to bring him into the room of their darkest moment.

Here again, we see a door closed while healing happens, like in the story of the Shunammite woman's son. This time Jesus only lets in three disciples (Peter, James, and John) and the girl's parents. He picks up her cold hand and says, "'My child, get up!' Her spirit returns, and at once she stands up"(v. 54-55).

When we think all hope is lost or that a relationship or situation is dead, we need to bring Jesus into the room anyway. Let him say to the dead situations and broken places in you the same thing he did to that girl—GET UP! He wants to restore our spirits and heal the dead things we're trying to live without.

We may have well-meaning people in our lives that tell us there's no point in asking for Jesus to redeem something or revive something in our lives. Maybe they're afraid we'll be disappointed or get our hopes up for nothing, but that's not how God works.

When the voices of fear and doubt try to tell us it's over and there's no point, we have to listen to God whispering, "Do not fear; only believe and _____ will be healed." There is nothing in our hearts or lives that is so dead God can't make it right. We just have to believe He can heal and let Him into our darkness.

Get the Glue:

- What is God trying to heal in your life that you've written off as dead? (Maybe it's a relationship, or a part of yourself you don't think can be restored, or a dream you've given up on ever happening. Identify it, so you can let God into it again.)

- Are you ready to reach out to Jesus for healing? Or are you still trying to heal yourself?

- What lies of fear and doubt do you need to let go of in order to trust that Jesus wants to heal you and *will* heal you?

<u>Prayer:</u> *Jesus, there are things I'm too scared to hope for anymore, things I've failed to fix over and over. Most days I've just accepted that my issues will always be my issues and the parts of me that are dead will never be brought back to life. But I know that's not what you have for me. You want to heal my faith and my heart. I'm reaching out for you with the faith I have, and I trust that Your power will make me whole again. When I am afraid, whisper to my soul, "Do not fear." Take my hand and pull me up from the darkness. Take the dead things in my life, and make them right.*

CHAPTER 8:

IT'S TOO LATE

FOR HEALING

John 11:1-44 [1]

We don't always picture Jesus as someone with friends. He was just the guy in the robe preaching on the side of the hill, right? Wrong. Jesus had friends, people he had dinner and hung out with. One of them was a man named Lazarus. Lazarus wasn't some random guy who'd heard about Jesus or met him once at the temple. He and Jesus loved each other.

One day while Jesus is out of town, Lazarus' sisters, Mary and Martha, send someone to tell Jesus, "Lord, the one you love is sick" (v.3). They didn't have to use his name; they knew Jesus would know it was Lazarus. At some point in life, you've likely received a similar phone call from someone you love. They usually start with something like, "The doctor says it's _____."

In this case, they weren't just telling Jesus so he could come say his goodbyes. They were hoping that he would do what they'd seen him do for so many others and heal his sickness.

Jesus tells the messenger, "This sickness will not end in death. It will be for God's glory..." (v. 4). That sounds like great news to take back to Mary and Martha! The passage reaffirms "Jesus loved Martha, Mary, and Lazarus. *Yet* he stayed where he was two more days" (v. 5-6).

When he finally decides it's time to go see Lazarus, he gets pushback from the disciples. They're afraid that it will be dangerous for Jesus to go back to Bethany because last time he was there the people tried to stone him. It seems like Jesus' disciples are trying to look out for him, but Jesus didn't share their fear. He's still the savior willing to leave the ninety-nine to find the one. Jesus is not afraid to step into the darkness to heal us. He is the light that walks into our darkness to draw us out.

He simply tells the disciples that their friend Lazarus is sleeping, and he's going to wake him up. His disciples weren't picking up what Jesus was putting down and figured if he's asleep, then he'll wake up. So Jesus turns to them again (I imagine with an eye roll), and says, "Lazarus is dead,

> **Jesus is not afraid to step into the darkness to heal us.**

and for your sake I am glad I was not there, so that you may believe. But let us go to him" (v. 14-15).

Lazarus' sisters' request for healing was grounded in an understanding of Jesus' love for them. Maybe they thought that meant they could demand Jesus follow their plans. After all, they'd made countless meals for him and sacrificed to support his ministry. But maybe that's the exact same reason Jesus decided to use them for a bigger purpose and bigger miracle than they would've imagined.

Our sacrifices for Jesus don't guarantee us our preferred timing and outcome from him. We may not like that, but it's because God's plans are bigger than our demands.

Jesus promised Lazarus' sickness wouldn't *end* in death because God was going to get glory from his story. There may be people or things in our lives that die, but that is not the end of the story. Death doesn't determine the end. Only God does.

When it seems like Jesus isn't answering us immediately or moving on our timeline, we need to know it is not because he loves us any less. It means he's asking us to wait for a better answer, a bigger miracle, than what we'd plan for ourselves. Though the feelings of helplessness and frustration while we wait aren't easy, the waiting isn't a cruelty or a wasted time. God is using it for a purpose we may not be able to see while we're waiting. There is learning to be done and faith to be grown while we wait.

If you're like me, I usually picture myself as Martha or Mary in this story, waiting for Jesus to heal someone I love. But we are also Lazarus. There are some gifts God has given us that we're not using. There are some parts of ourselves that we've been hiding out of hurt, and we've hid them for so long, we think they're dead. There are some dreams we failed to reach so many times we've convinced ourselves we don't want them anymore.

> There is a thin line between sadness and anger, and both are present when we're grieving a loss.

What if the things we think are dead in our lives are just things we've let go to sleep? What if we asked God to show up in those places and bring them back to life?

꘏꘏꘏

When Jesus arrives at Bethany, he "finds Lazarus has been in the tomb four days" (v. 17). He already knew this was the case because He's God! Bethany is less than two miles from Jerusalem, where Jesus was when he got the news. If that doesn't frustrate you, I don't think you're being honest.

As I read the story, I'm frustrated for Mary and Martha because Jesus knew Lazarus' state and knew how close he was, yet he didn't stop what happened. There is a thin line between sadness and anger, and both are present when we're grieving a loss.

Mary stays inside the house with other people who are there to mourn. Martha is hot with rage. She sees Jesus coming and goes out to give him a piece of her mind. She doesn't try to hide her anger from him or mince words. She says, "if you had been here, my brother would not have died" (v. 21). But she also doesn't try to take the problem out of his hands either. In her pain, she still clings to a shred of hope and says, "I know that even now God will give you whatever you ask" (v. 22).

Jesus speaks the impossible. "Your brother will rise again" (v. 23). Her logical mind can't comprehend anything other than Lazarus would rise again in eternity. He explains further, "I am the resurrection and the life. Whoever believes in me, though he dies, yet shall he live" (v. 25-26). When he asks if she believes that, all Martha gets out is, "I believe you are the Christ" (v. 27).

Sometimes it's hard in those moments to believe God for the impossible thing we really want most. Sometimes we believe who He is, but we fail to see who He is in our situation. Martha doesn't know what Jesus can or will do, but she calls Mary to come out of the house. She knows they both need to be with Jesus.

Mary's words are the same as Martha's when she reaches Jesus; "If you had been here, my brother wouldn't have died" (v. 32). But her posture is different. She falls at his feet weeping. Instead of asking her what she believes, he just weeps with her.

Jesus is deeply moved and walks to the tomb. He tells those standing there to take away the stone that was covering the mouth of the cave.

Martha, true to her form, doesn't want to open the tomb because she knows if he's been in there four days it's going to smell! Jesus goes back to what he said would be the point from the beginning: God's glory. He's not worried about the stank, so they roll the stone away.

Then he looks up to give God all the glory and says, "Father, I thank you that you have heard me. I knew that you always hear me, but I said this for the benefit of the people standing here, that they may believe that you sent me". He calls out loudly, "Lazarus come out!" (v. 41-43). And the dead man comes out with full mummy wrap still around him. Jesus tells them to unwrap his grave clothes so he can go free. If that's not a mic drop moment, I don't know what is.

Maybe you know exactly what it feels like when God could have done something about a situation in your life, but he didn't. You watched a loved one die while you prayed for healing. You watched a relationship crumble while you prayed for restoration. You watched a dream die while you prayed for success. So what do we do when this happens? We grieve.

There's nothing wrong with grieving; it's a part of life. Jesus wept even when he knew the outcome would get better. He may have us in a waiting season, but he's also sitting with us while we're weeping in that season. We can't stay in that grieving place permanently though. We have to take our pain, anger, fear, and hurt to Jesus.

If Mary had stayed in the house sulking in her grief and anger when Jesus called for her, she would have missed the miracle. Only when we are willing to get close to Him will we see His healing power work.

We don't know entirely where Martha's heart was at when she saw Jesus coming four days too late, but the two words that she utters "even now," are the seeds of faith that lead to a miracle. When we've experienced the death of something or someone, our human perspective tells us things are over and hopeless. We can't see a solution or a way to fix it. That's when we have to cling to the "even now."

God always does more than we ask or imagine (Eph. 3:20), *if* we put our dead things into His hands. Resurrection is God's way of healing after our timeline has run out. We've seen this with Jairus' daughter and the Shunammite's son already.

> Resurrection is God's way of healing after our timeline has run out.

We think healing stops being possible when someone or some part of us dies, but God's healing timeline doesn't stop there. We may want Jesus to fix our problem before it's dead, but He wants to resurrect it after it's dead. He gets all the glory for that. When we feel our heart is too broken to be whole or too dead to be restored, that is just the place for resurrection to start.

You may be thinking, "That sounds nice, but my loved one is already gone. They are in heaven. Now what?" First, thank you for even reading this chapter and not skipping over it. Second, you're not wrong! If they knew Jesus, I believe they are with Him in heaven as you're reading this. But that's not where resurrection has to stop.

Jesus wants to resurrect dead things in our lives on this side of heaven too. Our life story is to be a testimony to the world of his resurrection, but that means things in our life are going to die. It may be a person, a dream, or a job that dies. The way He chooses to resurrect it may be physically, like He did Lazarus, or the resurrection may come in Him bringing us back to life after we experience a heartbreak we think will kill us too.

No matter how He does it, the resurrection in our lives isn't just for us. Jesus raised Lazarus, not just for him, but for the sake of the disciples and those watching. Lazarus can't be quoted anywhere in scripture, but his life was an unspoken sermon going from death to life to freedom.

Resurrection is followed by an unbinding process. God will resurrect dead things in our lives: dead relationships, dead dreams, dead parts of our souls. But if we don't unbind our mindsets, habits, and expectations of death, we won't be able to walk in freedom.

Lazarus had to have help peeling off the strips of cloth they'd wrapped his body in. We also need a community where we can help unravel the past off of each other and tear off the things still binding us. We need people in our times of death who will lead us back to Jesus, even if they're hurting themselves. We can't keep the dead things in our lives hidden for fear of the mess and stink we don't want others to notice. We must be willing to roll back the stone.

When it's too late for healing, and there are dead things in our life, it's time for a different kind of healing-resurrection.

Get the Glue:

- If you were Lazarus, would you have been mad Jesus let you die or would you be grateful he let it happen so you could experience resurrection instead of healing? Are there places in your life where you need to start looking for resurrection instead of sitting in anger that healing didn't happen?

- What dead things have you been hiding out of shame? Are you willing to roll back the stone and let Jesus restore them to life?

- What area of fear, pain, anger, or disappointment do you need to have an honest conversation with Jesus about? (Don't wait. He loves you, and He's always close.)

<u>Prayer:</u> *God, You give me beauty for my ashes, but You also don't just disregard the ashes. ² You sit with me when I'm broken, when I've lost more than it seems like I can bear. You calm my anxious heart and bind up all my wounds. But You don't leave me there. You resurrect what I've written off as dead and work miracles I've stopped believing You for. All the outcomes I didn't like or understand, I'm trusting You with, even now. Today I'm rolling back the stone on all my pain and failure. I need You to call the dead things in me back to life. Peel back what's keeping me bound. Make me whole again. I want You to get all the glory in my story.*

CHAPTER 9:

I'M TIRED OF THE TAKING

Genesis 37, 39-50 [1]

Joseph's story is a very well known one. We remember it because it's filled with more trauma than a season of *Grey's Anatomy*. His trauma started young. He lost his mom when she died giving birth to his little brother, Benjamin. That left his father, Jacob, grieving and created a host of drama between him and his half-siblings and step-moms.

It's clear there is tension between Joseph and his brothers in Genesis 37 when they get mad at Joseph's big mouth and tell their dad a story to make him look bad. But despite that tense environment, Joseph has an anointed imagination, and God speaks to him through dreams. His big mouth makes those big dreams threatening to his brothers though.

When he tells them about a dream he has where they are all bowing down to him, they hit a breaking point. Gone are the days of tattle-telling to dad about

Joseph. They're going to handle things their own way. (Cue the sinister music...)

One day Jacob sends Joseph to check on his brothers who are off tending the livestock. He finally finds them, and they are not happy to see him. The first brilliant idea thrown around is to kill him, but God has one of his brothers, Reuben, looking out for him. He chimes in with a little reason and says, "Let's not take his life... Throw him into the cistern instead" (37:21-22).

As their spontaneous plan unfolds, they take his robe and throw him in the hole. I can only imagine his kicking and screaming as he yells, "Why are you doing this to me? This isn't funny guys! Get me out!" Then Judah pipes up with a new plan.

He wants to sell Joseph to some slave traders passing by instead of letting him die in the well. It's still a cruel plan, but he rationalizes it because at least they won't be killing him. They take Joseph's freedom and his home by selling him off. Then they try to cover it up by putting goat's blood on the fancy jacket they took and showing it to their dad to fake Joseph's death.

That added a whole new wave to this poor father's grief. And in his grief, Jacob goes off and does some pretty horrific things with women, but that's a story for another time.

Meanwhile, Joseph ends up sold into the foreign country of Egypt to a man who's working for

Pharaoh. In this man Potiphar's house, Joseph starts trying to make the most of the situation, or maybe just working hard to survive.

He is so successful that he ends up running Potiphar's house, only to have his integrity taken and thrown in the dirt when Potiphar's wife tries to entice Joseph and then falsely accuses him of rape! His minimal freedom is once again taken when he's imprisoned for this crime he didn't commit.

As this scene in the story unfolds in Genesis 39, seven times it says "God was with Joseph" and he has "favor" or "blessing." In the midst of what felt like more unfair taking and more pain, God was orchestrating things for Joseph's good. While in prison, Joseph still uses the gift God gave him and helps others interpret their dreams.

One of those people is a cupbearer to the king. The only thing Joseph asks of him in return is that when he's released he remembers Joseph and mentions him to Pharaoh. Does he? No. He forgets Joseph. Once again, Joseph is taken for granted and remains in prison, at least for now.

Two years later, Pharaoh has a dream he can't make heads or tails of, and the cupbearer finally remembers Joseph! After Joseph interprets the Pharaoh's dream, he's not only released from prison, but he's put as second in command in all of Egypt. What amazes me is that Joseph has kept his faith in God through all of this. His remarks to Pharaoh tell us as much.

He says things like, "God will do it," "God revealed it to me," and "God has shown me" (41:25, 28, 32). He could easily decide it's up to him to get out of this situation on his own and try to take all the responsibility and credit. But he doesn't. He knows God's hand is still on him, and God has given him this gift for a special reason.

The amount of trauma Joseph experiences in just the first part of his story is incomprehensible for most of us. He starts out life feeling abandoned and lost after losing his mother, and when he's sold into slavery that had to have multiplied his pain.

So much has been taken, and yet the pain of the aftermath is sometimes worse than the initial loss. Losing someone or something is one thing, but the reality of being a single parent, the anxiety you lay awake with at night, or the finances that seem to drown you are another level of pain.

Right when Joseph feels like he's starting to get ahead, a toxic person accuses him and throws him in prison. He must be getting tired of the toxicity and getting used. Pastor Jerry Flowers defines toxicity as "anything or anyone that distracts or disrupts your evolution by poisoning your heart with trauma."[2]

Some of us were hit with trauma in childhood, and our memories are fraught with pain. Some of us have normalized trauma to the point that we see adapting as healing. We may have adjusted to self-hatred, to settling, to depression, or to just surviving, but we weren't made to bleed our whole lives.[3]

Joseph had a dream and then went through the pain of betrayal, undeserved blame, abandonment, and captivity. He watched as dreams came to pass of those he'd helped, probably wondering when God was going to fulfill the dream he'd given him. But God was working even through the trauma.

> God plants dreams in our hearts because He knows we'll go through things that break us.

That dream He'd given Joseph was a picture of what he'd receive if he didn't give up. God plants dreams in our hearts because He knows we'll go through things that break us. The dream is not one more thing than can be taken from us. It's God's promise of what He's trying to make us into. No one can take that dream, but we can give it up if we aren't willing to go through the healing process.

A heart that is not rehabilitated will keep you from living the life you could have lived. Joseph may have made the right call lots of times and kept the faith in tough situations (which I give him major props for), but God knew his healing process wasn't through yet.

🔲🔲🔲

After thirteen years of being enslaved or imprisoned, it starts to look like things are turning around for Joseph. While he's in charge of running

Egypt, he gets a gorgeous new robe and gold chains, which are quite an upgrade from the robe that had been taken from him. God is not only a God of restoration, but when He restores He gives us a new version that's even better than before.

Joseph spends seven years preparing for the 7-year famine he predicted from Pharaoh's dream. He stores up so much grain, it's only described as "beyond measure" (41:49).

He also starts a family with the priest's daughter. Their first two sons' names are proof of the work God is doing in his heart. One means "God has made me forget my trouble," and the other means "God has made me fruitful in the land of my suffering" (41:51-52). This is what healing looks like. Your past pain no longer defines you, and you can see how God has given you victory in the places of your defeat.

It took thirteen years for God to turn what was taken from Joseph into something he could pour out as blessings to others. But God wasn't just using Joseph to help save the people from a famine, He was working in his heart during those thirteen years too.

All that heart work was in preparation for Joseph to face the darkest parts of his past—the deepest pains he'd ever experienced. While Egypt prepared for a famine, God was preparing the biggest miracle yet.

Joseph's brothers were out of food in Israel and on their way to Egypt. When Joseph's brothers make it to Egypt, his trauma is triggered. His brothers don't recognize him, and he certainly doesn't trust them. Joseph is governor in Egypt, meaning he's in control of who gets grain. His brothers bow down to him, but Joseph treats them like strangers and is short with them. He asks, "Where do you come from?"

They tell him they just came to get food, but he accuses them of being spies three times. He throws them all in prison for three days. Then he says he'll send back food with them if they leave one brother behind while they go get Benjamin (who had stayed home) and bring him back. This is a hostage situation.

The brothers start talking it over, and from their conversation it's clear they haven't healed either. They still feel guilty over selling Joseph and say, "Surely we are being punished because of our brother. We saw how distressed he was when he pleaded with us for his life, but we would not listen" (42:21). Then Reuben starts accusing the others and saying it's their fault.

Joseph overhears their conversation and has to turn away while he cries. He gathers himself, decides Simeon will be the brother who stays as a hostage, and has him tied up. Joseph orders the brothers' bags to be filled with grain and the silver they'd brought to pay for it put back in the bags too. This wasn't a kind gesture or Joseph's way of saying the grain was free. It was a plant, a test.

When the brothers open their sacks on their way back home, they flip out. They know they've been framed and will face major consequences if they show back up in Egypt looking like thieves. Jacob is beside himself when they tell him the story. At first he refuses to let Benjamin go back with them for fear he'll die too, but eventually they get desperate for food and he has no choice.

The same brothers who sold Joseph into slavery promise their father they will guard Benjamin's life with their own. They load up the best gifts they have and double the silver to take back with them and head back to Egypt.

As soon as Joseph sees them coming with Benjamin he tells his assistant to take them to his house and prepare a big lunch so they can eat together. His brothers have no idea what's going on and are terrified they're being taken as slaves. They confess everything to Joseph's assistant and tell him they've brought back twice the silver.

He doesn't take their silver. He just says, "It's all right. Don't be afraid. Your God and the God of your father has given you treasure in your sacks; I already received your silver" (43:23). The brothers clean themselves up and get the gifts together for when Joseph comes to eat, hoping to make a good impression.

Joseph only makes it through two small-talk questions about his father and his younger brother Benjamin before having to excuse himself to cry again. He washes his face and comes back to eat, but he eats alone.

Joseph tells the servants to give Benjamin five times as much food as the other brothers so he can watch to see if they still harbor the same jealousy and bitterness they used to have for him. They all enjoy a big dinner and drinks, and then Joseph sends them on their way home. He still had one more test for them though.

He'd had a servant plant a silver cup in Benjamin's bag to make it look like he'd stolen it. When they get a little ways down the road, he sends someone to "check it out." Of course, the cup is found in Benjamin's bag. When they are told Benjamin will have to be a slave because of his crime, Judah offers himself as a replacement, and they all beg Joseph to let Benjamin go home. They tell him if Benjamin doesn't return home, their father won't make it. And Joseph loses it.

Maybe it's because he never fully faced his family's betrayal, maybe he's been pretending it didn't happen, or maybe he's just realizing the vision God gave him all that time ago is finally coming true.

He blurts out, "I am Joseph!" and they freeze in fear. He tells them to come close and pours out his heart saying, "Do not be angry with yourselves for selling me here, because it was to save lives that God sent me ahead of you" (45:5). Three times he repeats "God sent me." He invites all of them to get their families and his father and come live in Egypt to ride out the famine. Then he hugs and kisses all of them as he weeps.

Joseph's whole family acquires the best of the land, not because they earned it, but because God was faithful to the promise he gave Joseph. Jacob thought he lost Joseph at seventeen, but now thirteen years later, God has brought them back together. In a time when all of Egypt is barely surviving, not only does Jacob get to see Joseph again, but he also gets to meet his grandkids.

We may never be able to imagine the ways God will restore what was taken from us, but we can trust that He *always* restores even beyond what we could imagine. God healed slower than Joseph may have liked, but it was to give Joseph time to grow in character and perspective before being confronted with those who'd hurt him. God healed as Joseph forgave. As Joseph healed from his broken past, God used him to mend his broken family.

Healing is something that's still happening long after we think it's over. It requires us to continually come back to God when we're triggered. That's the only way God can make us whole. We will all have dark parts come to the surface as we heal. As Steven Furtick points out, "Every person and every process has a dark part."4

If you don't deal with the dark part, you'll never get to the good part though. Sometimes that dark part we have to get through is our own mind. Maybe God was waiting for Joseph to get to the good in his mind before he made his life good. To have real intimacy, you've got to go through insecurity (the dark part).

> Sometimes that dark part we have to get through is our own mind.

Sometimes you'd rather take a pill, have a drink, leave a relationship, or pretend it's all fine than go *through* the dark part to get to real connection. You have to be seen to connect, and being seen takes shining the light on the dark parts of us.

Throughout the story we see God shine a light on the dark, broken places of Joseph and his brothers' hearts. First they try to cover the darkness of shame by lying about it. Then they try to fix it themselves by paying back twice the silver. But that's not how grace works. God places treasure in our jars of clay. When we break and fail to repay him for our wrongs, he pours out more and more grace.

Jesus' grace heals us when we accept his salvation, and yet we are still heal*ing* by His love. It's both a one-time moment and a process.

God also showed them the light of forgiveness. Not only did Joseph have to find a path to forgiving his brothers, but they also had to come to a place where they could forgive *themselves* for betraying him. There may be places of dark unforgiveness within us that need to be healed. Just remember, you can't forgive what you won't face and feel.

Numbing the pain or avoiding the people only makes the pain worse when you finally feel it, because our silent tears carry the loudest pain.[5] It's in the dark season of wrestling for our healing and freedom that we find out what God is doing within us, not because of

> Jesus' grace heals us when we accept his salvation, and yet we are still heali*ng* by His love. It's both a one-time moment and a process.

the answers we get but because of the questions we ask.

I'm sure Joseph had some massive questions for God during those dark years. But later, after Joseph's father is gone, he's able to say to his brothers, "You intended to harm me, but God intended it for good" (50:20). This isn't some sugar-coated answer Joseph wakes up and receives one day. He's had to work through his painful reality for years.

God has to give us His perspective before we can see what was taken *from* us as pieces He was working together *for* us. From His perspective, something isn't good based on how we feel while it's happening. He calls it good based on whether it serves His purpose. God doesn't say "it's all good" and dismiss our pain and trauma, but He does promise it's *going* to be good.

God was planning for the deliverance and saving of Joseph's brothers while they were selling him into slavery. God's redemptive grace is always planning for our rescue while we're busy breaking his heart. Just like the evening comes before morning, God starts good while it's still dark.

Everyone stops with Joseph's story after the first thirty years, but the last one hundred were the best part. He gets to see his great-great-great-grandchildren born and sit them on his lap.

When you're tired of what other people or your own past has taken from you, trust that God will restore it all to you. But for healing to happen, He has to restore what's within you.

Get the Glue:

- Are there traumatic or toxic memories from your past that you need to rehab from? (Shame or blame are not the goal here, just identifying what needs to be faced.)

- What dark places of your own soul have you tried to numb or avoid? What is one step you can take to start bringing them into the light?

- How can you begin to let God shift your perspective so that you can see what's good now instead of waiting until after it's gone?

Prayer: *Jesus, you know everything I've been through and every dark part of me. But you're not scared of my mess. You are the light. I'm done hiding my broken heart behind a big smile. Help me to get honest about my pain so I can start to heal. When I'm triggered by my trauma or tempted to listen to the toxic voices in my head, pursue me with Your grace. Meet me in the wrestling and questions I fight in the dark. Give me faith to see you are working it all for my good, even before it looks good. My future is not determined by my past, but by the working of Your hands. Thank You, Jesus, for restoration.*

CHAPTER 10:

FROM TRAUMA TO
TRIUMPH

John 18:15-27, 20:19-23 & 21:1-19 ;
Luke 22:49-62; Acts 12:1-17 [1]

You can taste the tension in the air. Jesus knows he's about to face execution on the cross, but instead of hiding or running he goes to the top of a mountain to pray.

In John's account of the story, five verses are spent recording what Jesus prayed for himself and twenty are spent recording his prayer for the disciples and all believers. It was clear that his heart wasn't focused on his own pain, but on them.

Into that beautiful olive grove, walk perfectly timed soldiers and a traitor named Judas, all looking for Jesus. Jesus knows why they are there and goes out to them voluntarily. He tells them who he is. No mugshot needed.

There is a tense exchange between Jesus and the soldiers. He tells them he's the guy they're looking for, and at first they back up. Maybe they thought he must be crazy if he's turning himself in or maybe they

> ...the sad part is even his best efforts aren't enough to stop his worst fears from happening or prevent his pain.

recognized he had authority that stopped them in their tracks. He tells them who he is again and says to let the disciples go.

That's when Peter steps up. He isn't going to walk away and let Jesus be taken. Fear, anger, or a protective instinct kick in, and he swings his sword and cuts off a soldier's ear. Why does he even have a sword when they just came to the garden to pray? It seems like Peter's the guy who's always ready for a fight or willing to defend those he loves.

Part of me wants to give him props for being the only one to try and save Jesus. The other part of me says, "What are you thinking, Peter? We know you weren't aiming for his ear! You could've made this situation so much worse than it already is!" Regardless of his motivations or whether you'd prosecute Peter in court, the sad part is even his best efforts aren't enough to stop his worst fears from happening or prevent his pain.

Jesus picks up the man's ear and puts it back on his head, like it's an ear on a potato head (Luke

22:50-52). Here Jesus is trying to fulfill his biggest purpose on Earth, something that wasn't going to be easy, and he's having to do miracles to cover for Peter's mistakes.

Peter's a wreck of emotions as he and another disciple follow behind Jesus who is brought to the high priest's house. To make matters worse, Peter can't even get into the priest's courtyard when they arrive. The other disciple has to go in and get permission from the girl on duty for Peter to come through the gate. Once he's in, the girl on duty asks if he's Jesus' disciple, and he replies, "I am not" (v. 17).

He stands for a while with the servants, warming himself by a fire. (That fire will be important later.) A second person asks him if he's Jesus' disciple, and again he denies knowing him. Then a relative of the man whose ear he'd cut off, who'd *seen* him in the olive grove, asks if he's a disciple. A third time, he denies Jesus. A rooster crows, and it all comes back to him.

The words of Jesus race through his mind, "Will you really lay down your life for me?" The truth is before the rooster crows, you will disown me three times." (John 13:38) And in that same instant, Jesus turns and locks eyes with Peter. Peter breaks down. He walks outside and weeps. He couldn't have been more ashamed and disappointed in himself. In that shame and pain, he runs.

Trauma can make you question who you are. In the garden that night, Peter lost the one person he'd built his life around. Trauma. He gets desperate to fix it, and commits an act of violence. More trauma. He watches helplessly from the outside as Jesus stands on trial, and in his fear he denies who Jesus is, betraying himself by doing so. Even more trauma. That repeated trauma made him feel weak and question who he was.

We all respond to trauma in different ways. Some of us blame others and lash out in anger. Some of us try to numb the pain. Others blame themselves and don't want to face the pain so we run. And most of us pile on shame.

> **There is no joy without facing the pain for what it is.**

From the first mention of shame in scripture with Adam and Eve, there is no mention of God shaming us. It's our own hearts that condemn us. Once we as humans had the knowledge of good and evil, it became easy for us to point at ourselves and deem ourselves "bad." BUT "God is greater than our hearts" (1 John 3:20, NIV), which is why we need His grace and power at work in us to overcome our own shame, regret, pain, and trauma.

Our own hearts will never be enough. God "already knows everything" (1 John 3:20, NIV). He even knew Peter would deny him three times before it happened. When we try to hide our shameful, broken pieces from Him, it's a waste of time. It's only delaying our own restoration and healing. There is no joy without facing the pain for what it is. If we can't be honest about the pain, that heavy blanket we're carrying will never lift.

When you're in that painful place of regret and disappointment, like Peter that Friday, you are blinded and it's hard to believe anything could get better or be restored. Steven Furtick says, "Accepting Jesus is the easy part. Accepting ourselves as holy and whole is the hard part. But if we don't accept ourselves as Jesus does, we've missed the point of salvation. The real challenge will be accepting God's process with us."[2]

∿∿∿

Cut to three days after Jesus' crucifixion. Jesus is raised to life, and his first appearance is to Mary Magdalene. He tells her to go share the news with the disciples *and Peter*. He's very specific about that. When Peter hears, he and John race to the tomb, only to find clothes and no Jesus. Where is he?

That evening as the disciples sit behind locked doors in fear, Jesus appears to them, scars and all. The disciples are all so excited to see him, but I can't imagine everything that must have been going through Peter's heart and mind at that moment. I'm sure part of Peter was truly happy and relieved to see him alive. But was there also an ashamed part of him that didn't know how to look Jesus in the eye?

Jesus talks to them that night about forgiveness, but Peter can't seem to forgive himself. He's seen his savior raised from the dead, but he's not out partying or celebrating. He's not calling up everyone he knows to tell them the good news. He's back doing what he did before he knew Jesus—fishing. Thomas, who also doubted Jesus recently, joins him.

Maybe they both felt unworthy to call themselves disciples anymore. But even as they're out on the boat sitting in their shame and isolation, Jesus is working miracles to redeem the place of Peter's failure.

You see, a few years ago, Jesus stood on that same shore and talked to Peter for the first time. Back then his name was Simon, and he'd failed to catch any fish all night. Jesus told him to go out into the deep one more time and "let down the nets for a catch" (Luke 5:4). When he did, he caught more fish than he could even handle.

Here Peter is again after a night of catching no fish, and he hears a voice from the shore say, "Hey guys, have you caught anything?" Then he tells them to throw their net on the right side of the boat and they'll catch something. This makes no fishing sense, but they do it anyway and again catch more fish than they can pull back up. That's the light bulb moment, and they realize it's Jesus. Peter doesn't waste any time. He jumps into the water and swims to shore.

On the shore Jesus has prepared another fire, just like the one from the courtyard. The fire before

Jesus' death was the place of Peter's greatest regret. He was confused by his situation, disappointed in Jesus, and disappointed in himself, so he walked.[3] This second fire is about to be the place of Peter's restoration.

He gave up and went back to what he knew, but seeing Jesus there on the shore he realizes Jesus still loves him and chooses him. And he can't get to him fast enough. Jesus' fire was a way to say, "I love you more than any failure, and you are still worthy." Peter watched as Jesus resurrected Jairus' daughter. Then God resurrected Jesus. And now Jesus is appearing to Peter to resurrect him too.

Jesus turns Peter's trauma trigger into a catalyst for hope and redemption.

No words are recorded at that fire, the text only says that Jesus' presence was close. After they finish eating, Jesus asks Peter three times, "Do you love me?" (21:15-17). It seems a little cruel to ask him three times, but I believe he was trying to remind Peter of something. The first two times he asks, he calls Peter by his old name, Simon. The third time he calls him by the name he'd given him—Peter.

Jesus was reminding Peter of who he was and that he'd been changed by God. His failures were the very things that qualified him for Jesus' assignment. It was not about his own works or efforts.

Craig Groeschel says, "As long as the focus is on you, you'll always be susceptible to shame. The only way to heal from shame is to put your focus on who God is and off of who you're not."[4] Peter may have felt that the trauma he'd been through would change his identity and how his life would end, but Jesus reminds him that the end hasn't changed.

Peter will die faithfully serving Christ, like Jesus told him in John 13. Our trauma does not have to keep us from the things Jesus has planned for us. We just have to choose which fire will define us: our biggest regret or Jesus' redemption.

Over and over, Peter dives in wholeheartedly, makes massive mistakes, and then feels unworthy and runs. Over and over, Jesus' love pursues him and restores him. Triumph over trauma is not a one-and-done thing, but something we must consistently let God do in our hearts over and over by His grace and love.

卐卐卐

Peter's dramatic story is far from over that day on the shore. He spends years boldly building the early church, and then one day he's picked up and put in prison as a PR stunt for King Herod. His fellow disciple, James, has already been killed for the same reason.

The night before his bogus trial, Peter is asleep, chained to two guards, when an angel appears. The angel smacks Peter to wake him up and tells him, "'Quick get up!' and the chains fall off Peter's wrists

(Acts 12:7). Then the angel tells him to get dressed and follow him.

"They pass by the first and second guards and come to the iron gate heading to the city. It opens for them by itself, and they go through it" (12:10). There is no indication Peter had the faith he'd be freed from prison. In fact, he is in such shock from the angel that he thinks he is dreaming the whole thing until he is outside the prison.

He immediately goes to Mary's house, the mother of John, because he knows the believers there have been praying for him. They're praying after having just lost James! A lot of us pray for things we no longer believe can happen or hope for things we really don't believe are possible. The faith of these believers to keep praying for miracles after loss is pretty impressive, but their faith may not be as perfect as we think.

When Peter comes to the door and knocks, a servant girl answers. She flips out that it's Peter and slams the door in his face while she goes to tell everyone he's there. They tell her she's crazy, and "it must be his angel" (12:15). It's easier for them to believe it's over and this is his angel than to believe he is free. Peter keeps knocking until they finally open the door. Then he tells them the story of how God sent an angel to rescue him.

For each of us there are prisons of trauma, depression, addiction, isolation, disconnection, and denial. When Peter was in prison it meant those who loved him couldn't get to him or help him, and the same is true for those in our lives trapped in emotional prisons. The effects extend beyond the person who is trapped.

There is someone who can reach inside any prison though—Jesus. Just like he sent rescue for Peter, he sends rescue when we're trapped in our own prisons.

Even after Jesus sends the angel to rescue Peter, it still takes his obedience to get out.

> Your path to freedom is already open, but you have to go through it. You have to do the hard work of healing, and trusting, and hoping again.

Think about the order of events in the story. Peter gets up, and *then* the chains fall off. Steven Furtick says, "Obedience creates freedom, freedom from having to know the outcome before you take a step. If Peter doesn't get up, the chains stay on. If he waits for the chains to fall off before he gets up, he'll never be free."[5]

Many of us would still be stuck in that prison because we wouldn't move until we knew the details of the plan. Peter got dressed even when the angel hadn't told him the destination yet. He also didn't try to take over the plan. He understood freedom isn't about self-indulgence or self-discipline. It's about love.

God's love was rescuing him, and he was coming into agreement with God's plan, step by step until he was free. God will do for you what you can't do for yourself—open the gate. But He won't do what you can do—walk through it. Your path to freedom is already open, but you have to go through it. You have to do the hard work of healing, and trusting, and hoping again.

It may be easier to believe it's over for you than to believe God can set you free from yourself. But don't give up hope. Peter's rescue came at the last hour and was not what anyone would have expected. Your story of rescue and freedom may come when it seems all hope is lost and come in a way no one would have predicted too. God will never stop healing our trauma, replacing our warped identities, and restoring our faith in Him.

Get the Glue:

- When Peter ran back to his boat, he was running from the people who could've made him face the truth of his pain. Are you being more loyal to your trauma than you are to those in your life trying to help you heal?

- Jesus is standing on the shore waiting to comfort and restore you in your pain. But are you listening for His voice? Is your heart ready to see Him waiting and working?

- What prisons are you trapped in? What does it look like for you to get up, let the chains fall, and walk through the open doors God has in front of you?

<u>Prayer:</u> *Jesus, I've responded in anger and fear when really my heart was hurting. I've closed myself off and run because I didn't want to face the pain. But today, I feel You taking me by the hand as the chains come off. You've been ready and waiting for me all this time. Ready to redeem me, restore me, and set me free. It's time for me to trust that Your love and grace are bigger than any trauma in my life. It's time to walk through the tough stuff and let You put me back together. Thank You for not walking away at my first fire or the second or the third. I know my heart will condemn me. When it does, set fire to my shame. You are greater than my messed up heart. Please hold me together in this process and show me step by step what freedom looks like.*

Chapter 11:

Your Head Can Block Your Heart's Healing

2 Kings 5 [1]; Mark 3:1-5 [2]

A "great man," "highly regarded," and a "valiant soldier..." (2 Kings 5:1) Naaman was all of these things, *but* he also had leprosy. He was a big shot in his career, *but* his skin was rotting away.

Everyone has a "but," and we're usually trying to cover it. Naaman iruns towards the battlefield every day as a commander, but internally he runs from something he can't avoid. He has people clapping for him after each army victory and looking up to him. On the battlefield he's covered with armor. But when he goes home at night, he can't even allow anyone to see him without his armor on.

He must feel like a fraud, like he is unseen and unknown. He's decided if anyone sees his spots they won't accept him or love him or admire him anymore. Maybe he became a soldier to have a reason to wear the armor and cover his skin. Or maybe he was used to fighting something within and needed to put a face to what he was feeling.

Naaman's been trying to cover it up and pretend it's not getting worse for a while now, but if he doesn't get help soon there's no telling what he'll lose... limbs, function, or even his life. That's when a young Israelite girl who's been taken captive offers a suggestion. She has no reason to help him; after all, he is largely responsible for her pain. Naaman is an enemy commander who took her and her people captive. Nonetheless, God gave her a special heart for him.

She tells Naaman about a prophet of God, named Elisha (the successor to Elijah), who has been known to heal people. This sounds promising to Naaman, but there is a lot of vulnerability and risk required for this plan. He has to trust the word of his servant girl, *and* he's got to expose his biggest secret to his boss, the king, in order to ask permission to go. But Naaman is desperate, so he risks it. Thankfully the king is understanding and even volunteers to write a letter to the King of Israel on Naaman's behalf.

We, like Naaman, become fighters to keep anyone from seeing our "but." We hide behind our abilities, our pride, our success, or our titles. All the while, our pain is spreading and eating us alive.

We're not meant to be at peace in our problems because peace is only found in Jesus. That discomfort is a fuel to get us through the pain to the miracle on the other side. If we get too comfortable with the problem, we'll never push through to the other side. If we get addicted to dysfunctional relationships, anxiety, and depression, we'll stay stuck in the problem.

> **If we get too comfortable with the problem, we'll never push through to the other side.**

And if we believe the lie that asking for help is weakness, we'll miss our healing. God wants to expose our "spots" to the Light, but what we do when they're exposed will determine whether or not we get healed.

卐卐卐

Naaman rolls up to the King of Israel's place like a true gangster. When he opens the trunk, he's got seventy-five pounds of silver and gold and a pile of nice clothes as gifts (or bribes) for the King. He wants to *attain* healing. When we need healing the most, we hide behind stuff too.

Naaman is used to being prepared, powerful, and persistent in what he does. He has a picture of what he thinks he'll need to do to get healing, and he's trying to make things happen. The problem goes back to verse 1 of the passage where it says, "the Lord gave him victory" (v. 1). His victory in battle wasn't won *by* him at all; it was won *through* God.

His healing would be no different and neither is ours. If we could fix our own problems, there would be no need for a savior. If we think we're both the problem and the solution, the failure and the fixer, we're going to put a lot of pressure on ourselves. That's when people self-sabotage because then it seems like they can "control" their failure and relieve the pressure.

Naaman's got a lot riding on this plan. Failure isn't an option.

The King of Israel opens the letter that Naaman's king has written, which asks the King of Israel to heal Naaman. The King of Israel flips out, tears his clothes, and screams, "Am I God?" (v. 7). He immediately goes into fear mode because he's presented with a task he knows he can't do and accuses the King of Israel of trying to pick a fight.

His trauma from years of war has trained him to think everything is a fight. That's exhausting. If what you went through isn't healed by what Christ did for you, you'll inflict the present moment with the pain of your past. You'll treat opportunity like an

> **If we think we're both the problem and the solution, the failure and the fixer, we're going to put a lot of pressure on ourselves.**

attack. You'll spend time fighting things or people God sends into your life when they are meant to be opportunities.

Thankfully, what triggered fear in the king triggered faith in Elisha. Where the king sees opposition, Elisha sees opportunity. He's trusting God to do the impossible through him yet again, and tells the King to send Naaman to him. Elisha wasn't concerned about not having the power to fix the situation because he knew it wasn't about his power, but God working through him.

It took some faith for Naaman to even take his whole crew to see Elisha. He didn't know Elisha and didn't believe in Elisha's God, but why not try? When he gets there, Elisha doesn't even come to see him. A messenger comes out front and says, "Go, wash yourself seven times in the Jordan and your flesh will be restored and you will be cleansed" (v. 10).

That's it?! Naaman storms off in anger. He's offended that Elisha would send a messenger out, disgusted that he's supposed to get into the Jordan (a notoriously muddy river in enemy territory), and disappointed because none of his expectations have been met.

Sometimes we're so tired of being broken, we start throwing the broken pieces of ourselves. We lash out at people who get too close. We take out our pain on those who try to help pick up the pieces. Like Naaman, we look up and realize we're hurting others who got close in an effort to help.

He's about to miss the opportunity to be healed because he goes away instead of going in. He thought he knew how this healing would go, and it almost got in the way of it happening. He's standing in front of a miracle and his head gets in the way.

> Sometimes we're so tired of being broken, we start throwing the broken pieces of ourselves. We lash out at people who get too close. We take out our pain on those who try to help pick up the pieces.

The directions are simple and he even gets to keep his gold and silver! His pride is triggered when he sees the method for healing as beneath him. When your heart is triggered by pride, you try to write your own prescriptions. "I thought" are the two words standing between him and healing (v. 11).

That's when his servants encourage him to do what seems too small to secure healing. Naaman reluctantly goes to the river and starts dipping in the water. Maybe his spots disappeared a little bit more each time he dipped, or maybe nothing changed until dip number seven. We don't know.

What we know is God cleansed him and restored his skin to the point it looked like a child's, and Naaman exclaimed, "there is no God in all the world except in Israel" (v. 15). God didn't put makeup on his spots to hide them or give Naaman a cream to numb the pain. God's not in the business of smoothing over our current pain. He restores us and cleanses us from pain we've been feeling since childhood. He makes us new. God's goal wasn't just healing Naaman's skin but building faith in his Healer.

Not everything has to be a big fight or a great feat of strength. Sometimes our biggest miracles will be in humbling ourselves to do the small things God says will bring us healing. Naaman had a great plan, but that's not the way it went. God's ways are higher than our ways, which means our expectations may not always be met. If they were, they'd never be exceeded.

We can't use our charm or charisma to cover our cracks.[3] We can't isolate and try to solve our own problems our own way. We can't lash out or withdraw in fear. And we can't let our stubborn pride tell us to walk away when our plans fail. We have to learn, like Naaman, to come into God's presence and say, "I don't want to be right. I want to be healed."

🏵🏵🏵

In the New Testament we find another story of a man who risks everything to be healed. His name isn't listed, nor does he have a powerful title, like commander Naaman. But he has a withered hand, something he's incapable of healing himself. One day he comes to the synagogue because he hears Jesus will be there. That's already a massive risk because the man is considered "unclean" and can be stoned just for showing up.

> **We have to expose our pain and shame to be healed.**

Jesus sees the man and says, "Come here" (Mark 3:3). While all the glaring eyes of the religious leaders look on, Jesus tells him, "Stretch out your hand". As soon as he stretches it out, "his hand is completely restored" (v. 5).

Notice, Jesus doesn't tell him which hand to stretch out. He could've easily held out the other hand that was whole. And many of us would! But instead he risks being kicked out, risks being shamed, in hopes of being healed. We have to do the same. We have to expose our pain and shame to be healed.

Shame tells us to hide, to cover, to be afraid of exposure. But shame doesn't just affect you. It makes you hide from everything and everyone in your life. It removes connection and vulnerability between people.[4] You weren't meant to stay in darkness and disgrace. It's not a fruitful place, no matter how hard you try to make things right.

Healing doesn't start in your head. It's not going to come from your stubborn pride, the stuff you try to hide, or even your best efforts to fix it. Healing will only come when your head gets out of the way and you get vulnerable. Brené Brown says, "Vulnerability sounds like truth and feels like courage. Truth and courage aren't always comfortable..." [5] But if you'll go from hiding things from God to hiding in God (Ps. 9:9), it'll change everything.

Get the Glue:

- What are you hiding? What are you trying desperately to cover up? What is it doing to you while you avoid exposing it?

- If your healing requires it, will you be willing to listen to someone who seems beneath you? Will you trust someone who shouldn't be trying to help you but is?

- Do you spend more time focused on God's sovereignty or your responsibility?

- Do you try to take on responsibility for fixing it all, holding it all together, or making it all work?

- What would freedom look like if you were to put the role of Healer back in His hands?

<u>Prayer:</u> *Jesus, it's scary to expose my flaws. It's hard sometimes to even own them to myself. But I know the longer I try to hide what's hurting me, the more damage it does. I'm tired of hurting and hoping no one notices. Give me the faith to trust in Your healing plan more than I trust the lies of my shame. Give me the strength to take small steps as You lead, even when I don't feel like it, even when I don't see an immediate change. You promise to restore and promise to redeem. That's all I have to know. You will be near my broken heart through every season of my healing (Ps. 34:18). Thank You for Your grace that covers all my darkest places.*

CHAPTER 12:

HEALING TRICKLES DOWN

Judges 6-8 [1]

Have you ever felt like your life was under attack? Like there were too many fires to put out at once? Like everyone needs everything from you all at the same time?

That's exactly where the Israelites sit. They are in hiding because their lives are under attack by cruel people named the Midianites. Every time the Israelites plant crops, the Midianites come through and take everything. Helpless and hungry, the Israelites are hiding in caves and cliffs just trying to make it.

In their hiding, they cry out to God for help. I'm sure they wanted God to swoop down, comfort them, and rescue them instantly. We certainly want that when life's crumbling around us. But God's first response is to show them, through the words of a prophet, how they got to this place.

They've gone from a place of deliverance out of Egypt to a place of desperation because they stopped listening to God. They are worshipping gods they can control, ones they make with their own hands. It wouldn't be easy to hear this, but if God didn't reveal how they got here they'd only repeat the same mistakes after He rescued them.

While the Israelites are asking God to deliver them, He goes to talk to a deliverer. It doesn't say God said anything back to the Israelites. He doesn't stop to talk to the problem; He goes straight to the answer.

God sends an angel to a man named Gideon. The angel tells Gideon, "The Lord is with you, mighty warrior" (6:12). There is *nothing* mighty or warrior-like about what Gideon is doing at this moment. He is hiding in a wine press, a big hole in the ground, threshing wheat, hoping the Midianites wouldn't see him.

Deafening silence is all he's heard in a long time. The kind of silence where you leave the TV on just to have some noise, where you turn on the music to fall asleep. Gideon witnessed unimaginable trauma against his people, his family, and his home. Standing there alone in that hole, all he feels is scared, defeated, and alone.

That's why the angel's first words remind him of who is with him and who Gideon is. Obviously, both are things he's forgotten or started to doubt because he doesn't say, "Thanks for the pep talk!" No, instead he responds honestly and unloads his doubt. He asks, "If the Lord is with us, why has all this happened to us? Where are all of His wonderful deeds from before?... The Lord has abandoned us and given us into the hand of Midian" (6:13).

He doesn't feel like God is with him. He doubts God, blames Him, and feels abandoned by the One he thought should've rescued them. God doesn't tell him off, shame him, or change his mind about using him. In fact, He doesn't even acknowledge his whining. The angel just says, "Go in the strength you have and save Israel out of Midian's hand. Am I not sending you?" (6:14).

I probably would've responded with something sarcastic, like, "Yea, sure. No problem. I'll go handle Midian right after I'm done with breakfast." But Gideon's first response is the obvious one, "How can I save Israel? I am the weakest in my clan, and I am the least in my family" (6:15).

Even if he is the strongest man or from the greatest family, he still doesn't have a shot to save a whole nation on his own! But that isn't the point. God isn't sending Gideon to do this because He knows how strong Gideon is and thinks he can handle it. God is sending him so that He can demonstrate His strength *in* Gideon.

In our weakness, GOD is strong. God also reminds Gideon that he's not sending him into this fight alone. He says, "I will be with you, and you will strike down the Midianites as if they were but one man" (6:16). Gideon is used to fighting alone and has forgotten that God never intended for it to be that way. God knew he would never experience victory that way.

> Gideon is used to fighting alone and has forgotten that God never intended for it to be that way.

Gideon, who's still not sold on this plan, asks God for a sign. God knows Gideon's faith needs to be rebuilt and is gracious enough to show him the signs a few times. Gideon is used to looking for reasons God isn't with him. He has a punch list of things that God hasn't done and reasons why God can't use him. I bet you have a similar punch list. I know I do.

What we see depends on what we're looking for. When Gideon starts to look for signs that God is with him, he realizes God has already been faithfully showing up in his life. He has protected him all this time, given him grain for his family, and kept his family together. God was even sitting in front of him! God is patient enough to show Gideon little signs over and over, even though he missed the big signs. God shows us His faithfulness over and over, but we have to be looking for it in the big and small things.

The angel of the Lord disappears. *Then* Gideon realizes it was an angel from the Lord. It isn't until after the angel of the Lord is out of sight that Gideon sees who he's been with. Then fear kicks in. His mind races with, "How could I have not seen this? Did I miss out? What if I screwed this up?" The Lord says to him, "Peace be to you. Do not fear; you shall not die" (6:23). I'm thinking he should have led the conversation with that!

Gideon builds an altar to remember what God showed him that day. Gideon doesn't want to forget the identity God had given him, but he is smart enough to know he'd need reminding in the future. He brings a sacrifice of unleavened bread, which represents God's faithfulness in Israel's past. Even though he doesn't feel like God was working in the present, he looked back to how faithful God was in the past in order to build his faith.

We need to put up physical reminders of God's peace and faithfulness so that we can remind ourselves of who HE is and who we are when the whispers of fear and shame and doubt come back. The battle hasn't even started yet, but God gives him peace that He will be with Gideon and there will be victory.

The moments where we say "yes" to the fight and God grants us peace I like to call "peace markers." This book is filled with my own peace markers where God spoke something I needed to hear right when I needed to hear it through a sermon, a song, a book, or a scripture. I hope this book can be a peace marker for you in your fight too.

God is patient with you in your process. He's patient with you in fear, poor decisions, and pain. Gideon had given up on God after seven years of tragedy, but God didn't give up on him. When God calls you, He calls you according to your potential.

> God is patient with you in your process. He's patient with you in fear, poor decisions, and pain.

Gideon could only see one day ahead and was just trying to survive, but God saw more for his life than that. God is ok with the space between who you are and who you'll become. When he looks at Gideon throwing wheat around in a wine press, He sees his desire to protect and provide for his family. Even while you're in hiding, he sees a fighter inside you.

Sometimes we're living hungry and in hiding because of circumstances outside our control, like illness or job loss, and other times it's because of our own choices. Our natural tendency in this place is to withdraw, hide, and suffer alone. We convince ourselves no one cares or understands. We don't ask for help because we think we shouldn't be in this place anyways.

Not only has Gideon decided to hide, but he's working way harder than he should to do a very simple thing—thresh wheat. You need wind to blow away the debris in the wheat and leave the part you can use. But there's not much wind in a wine press. It's a big hole insulated with brick or stone.

That's how it feels when we're hiding and trying to handle everything on our own. We're working even harder to make less progress. We're trying to fulfill a purpose, but we're swirling around in the mess. That's survival mode.

Holly Furtick, of Elevation Church, says, "God never wants us to live in hiding, to live with fear lurking around every corner, and scavenging for scraps of encouragement. We have to turn from survival mode to living out our faith as we fight to live."[2] We can't focus on *how* we got here, but we have to turn to *who* is with us and *where* He's leading us now.

> We can't focus on *how* we got here, but we have to turn to *who* is with us and *where* He's leading us now.

God will send a rescue when He knows our hearts are ready to receive it. Like Israel, we have to get low enough and tired enough of where we are to cry out to God. When we do, He always hears us. But usually our relief comes from an action He calls us to take.

I picture it like a father teaching a child how to swing on the monkey bars. He keeps telling us to reach out for the next bar and move one hand at a time. We may feel like we'll fall, but all the while our father is holding us. When God calls us to something we can't do ourselves, He prepares us along the way. We're never going to feel ready. We just have to move our heads out of the way of our hearts, and swing to the next bar.

卐卐卐

The first thing God calls Gideon to do as a warrior is a pretty ballsy move. He tells him to tear down the idols his father has put up and build an altar to God on top. He doesn't tell him to fight his dad or cut him off, but he does require him to tear down what was holding his family back.

God has to demolish the strongholds and lies in our mind before He can build something new or restore something that was taken. Otherwise, we'll have stuff in the way. Gideon has enough faith to do it, but he goes at night because he's still scared.

Even though he didn't know how his family would react, his first act of obedience pays off. His father stands up for him in the community, and the incident actually marks him with a name change. As Gideon continues to be obedient, God uses each step of faith to shape his identity.

The Midianites surround Israel, but God surrounds Gideon with His Spirit. It says, "But the Spirit of the Lord clothes Gideon, and he sounds the trumpet" to rally the troops (6:34). The armies of Israel gather together under Gideon's leadership. That's already a sign God is directing this! No one had any reason to follow Gideon from the winepress otherwise.

Even after he rallies the troops, he still struggles to rally enough faith for the fight. He asks God for two more signs using wool and fleece. God doesn't promise he'll always give us physical signs when he calls us to do something, but he does know what our hearts need. He's not above using even our day-to-day circumstances to multiply our faith if we just ask.

God prepares Gideon for battle by dwindling his men down from 32,000 to 300. I've never seen a military movie where this was the strategy! But God wasn't focused on building the strength of Israel's army. He was set on building the strength of the man from the weakest clan.

If he's our *only* shot at coming out alive, our ears are going to be wide open! And when he gives us the victory despite impossible odds, He will receive all the glory.

God sends Gideon and his 300 remaining men down into the valley to fight. They find more men and camels than they can even count, but God shows up for battle with Gideon like he promised. In true dramatic fashion that only God could pull off, they win the battle with 300 trumpets and some broken jars.

The battle isn't won because Gideon sits and waits for God to get rid of the enemy. He trusts what God has promised him, and he takes action. It's not possible for us to see a victory unless we do the same. Gideon's victory didn't just impact him. It helped free so many others from oppression. Judah Smith says, "You can't let your insecurity keep you from your healing because someone else's healing depends on it."[3] The things God calls you to are never just about you.

The fight is about more than defeating the Midianites. It is about Gideon fighting to see himself the way God

> **The things God calls you to are never just about you.**

does, as a mighty warrior, and restoring Gideon's faith in God. The battle isn't over that day either. Gideon begins an exhausting pursuit of the Midianites as they run. Not everyone he assumes will be on his side remains supportive, but he doesn't give up. He pursues God's purpose for him relentlessly.

When the battles are all over, the people try to give Gideon all the credit and ask him to rule Israel. But he refuses and says, "the Lord will rule over you" (8:23). He could have had a savior complex because God used him to rescue the people, but he never forgot it was only possible by *God's* work and not his own.

The battle we're in is God's to fight, but that doesn't mean we get to sit up in the stands and just watch the fight.[4] You are a warrior in your own right. You only have to have enough faith to take the first step, even if it's in the dark. Robert Madu says,

"Sometimes God has to work with us in the dark before we're brave enough to show others what He's doing in us."5

You only have to have enough faith to start, even if you're scared. If there's no fear, not much faith is required. Faith is work. It's grit. As the Spirit of God works through you, He will reform who you know yourself to be. He will sustain you in every battle.

Taking steps of faith may feel like you're walking into a valley. Leaving hiding to go fight for your future, and your children's future, may be scary. But staying in the hole alone forever is scarier. Taking steps forward in the healing process can feel like more than you can handle, but others are depending on you to heal.

Get the Glue:

- What is the internal tension you feel when God calls you forward? Is it guilt, fear, or insecurity? Are there thoughts of "I don't have enough to give," "I might fail," "I don't deserve it," or "I don't know how"?

- What does it look like for you to place the identity God's given you above your own insecurity?

- What patterns, tendencies, or sinful habits have you passed down through your family that God is calling you to tear down? (We can't keep doing things like they've always been done if the past pain of our families is keeping us from our purpose.)

- What battle is God calling you to fight for your future and those around you? Are you fighting it with Him or trying to fight it alone?

<u>Prayer:</u> *God, it's easier to be guarded than to step up and fight. It's easier to hide in my pain and shame than believe that victory is possible. But when You look at me, You don't see weakness and failure. You see a warrior. Please give me eyes to see myself the way You do. Give me signs, big and small, that remind me You're with me. Give me faith to see victory even in the valley. Grant me courage to fight for healing, not just for me, but for all those who will be affected by my life. Do more through my life than I could ask or imagine. One step at a time, one battle at a time, one victory at a time.*

HOLES IN WHOLENESS

If you go through life without knowing wholeness, you will operate about as well as a cracked vessel. Every time you're filled up, you'll be just as quickly drained. You will be confined to sitting on a shelf empty instead of experiencing the fullness of what you were made for.

As a broken piece of kintsugi pottery is restored, holes may be left after all the pieces are put in place. Some pieces are lost or smashed into dust. There is simply nothing to glue together.

We all have holes. Places we'll never be enough. Places of loss that took something from us. That's where we need the most glue and the brightest gold.

Will you let the love of God fill the holes where no piece is left? Will you let His grace cover the gaps between who you used to be and who He's making you into? Could those places where you feel most empty become the places of greatest beauty?

Imperfections are just the start of something new.1 You are not perpetually broken. You were made to be whole. You will know fullness again, all the way to the top.

CHAPTER 13:

EMPTY PLACES ARE WHAT

HE WANTS TO FILL

1 Kings 17:7-24 [1]; 2 Kings 4:1-7 [2]

Before the days of the big showdown on Mount Carmel, the prophet Elijah spends three years in the wilderness alone. He drinks from a brook and is fed by ravens. Picture a Harrison Ford like character with a scraggly beard and a crazy look in his eyes. He hasn't seen a shower or another person in far too long.

Then one day the brook dries up, and God tells him to go into a city named Zarephath. He promises Elijah that He will provide a widow there to give him food. I don't think the widow had gotten the notice in the mail that Elijah was coming though! He walks up to her at the town gate and asks for a little bit of water. As she's getting the hot mess Elijah a drink, he says, "Oh and please bring me a piece of bread".

That was too much. She says, "I have nothing baked, only a handful of flour in a jar and a little oil in a jug. And now I am gathering a couple of sticks that I may go in and prepare it for myself and my son, that we may eat it and die" (17:12). If I were Elijah, I would have felt so bad in that moment and immediately said, "I'm so sorry. I had no idea. Why don't I try to help you find some more food somewhere else?"

But that's not what Elijah does. He says, "Don't be afraid. Go home and do as you have said. But *first* make a small cake of bread for me from what you have and bring it to me, and then make something for yourself and your son. For this is what the Lord, the God of Israel says: The jar of flour will not be used up and the jug of oil will not run dry until the day the Lord gives rain on the land" (v. 13-14).

She goes home and does exactly what Elijah said. "So there was food every day for Elijah and for the woman and her family. For the jar of flour was not used up and the jug of oil did not run dry, in keeping with the word of the Lord spoken by Elijah" (v. 15-16).

This widow wrote herself off as over, and so had society. But God wasn't finished with her at all! Jeremy Foster points out, "God had directed her to that spot, but she didn't know the directions. God will orchestrate our paths to the places He wants to change us, even when we've given up hope."3

When Elijah goes to her and asks for bread, her first response is that she has nothing. She thought because she didn't have *enough* that she had *nothing* to offer. It wasn't nothing though; it was the something God wanted to use. Then she labels it as "a little." But God didn't need a lot to work with for a miracle. He needed her to give up the little she had.

What's not enough in our hands is more than enough in His. Sometimes we try to keep something

> **What's not enough in our hands is more than enough in His.**

little out of fear of failure. We put ourselves down because that's easier than risking opening up what we do have. No matter what we say to ourselves, God likes little. His Word proves it.

He used little Gideon and his little army to rescue Israel. He used a little servant girl to help Naaman find healing. And God had a plan for this widow's "little" too.

She may have had a little, but she needed a big miracle to save her family from famine and death. When Elijah meets her, she's operating in total survival mode. It may come across as selfish when she doesn't offer him any bread, but she was a mom who didn't want to give up the little she had to survive on. And yet that's exactly what God asks her to do—give up her little.

Notice Elijah's instructions are for her to make bread for him *first*. If she'd done what I would have been tempted to do, she would have made food for her and her son first and seen if there were leftovers for Elijah. And they would have died.

God always wants the firsts (or bests) in our lives; otherwise, there is no faith involved. If she hadn't been willing to give up the little she had in hopes that God would do something with it, there would have been no leftovers. Her surrender saved her *and* her child.

This was not a "they got my order wrong" kind of situation. It was life and death. So when Elijah tells her, "do not fear," I want to defend her. She has every reason to be afraid, and was probably afraid before Elijah ever got there, because she thinks she's about to die. But the very weight of her situation is also what releases her from her fear.

> God can do a lot with a little bit of faith, a little bit of hope.

If she didn't have enough but God asked for it anyway, God would have to be all that she needed. She needed help; it couldn't be all on her. Here is where she had to decide what would drive her actions—fear or faith.

Elijah gives her the instructions (go and make me bread) before the promise (it won't run out) for a reason. It is a test of her faith. A faith that can't be tested is a faith that can't be trusted. When she does obey Elijah, she doesn't get more oil and more flour. It just says what she had never ran out. It must not have been as "little" as she thought. God can do a lot with a little bit of faith, a little bit of hope.[4]

Each day as she makes bread, God is consistently growing her faith. Every day she gives Elijah the first piece and watches as God ensures there is still enough for her family. In verse seven God teaches her how to put something little in His hands because He knows by verse 17 she's going to have to put something much bigger in His hands.

Some time later her son dies. She watches him get worse and worse until there is no breath left in him. The first thing this grieving mom does is ask Elijah if it's her fault, if it's because of her sin. She still feels like the protection and provision for this family is all on her somehow, even though God has shown her over and over He is the one protecting and providing for her and her family.

Despite all her fear and guilt, she still has enough faith to hand the boy over to Elijah when he asks. Elijah takes him upstairs to his bed. Then he stretches himself out over the boy and cries out to God, "Have you brought tragedy on this widow...? O Lord my God, let this boy's life return to him! The Lord hears Elijah's cry, and the boy's life returns to him, and he lives" (v. 20-22).

God listens when we ask for healing, even when our cries start with questions about why this is happening. Great faith, faith that heals, is honest with God about the questions in our hearts but still trusts Him to restore, resurrect, and revive the dead things in us. Every time there's something in the way, faith sees it as a chance for Jesus to be the way maker.

卐卐卐

In 2 Kings 4 we meet a different widow who is also scrambling to save her family. She's lost her spouse and fears her children will be taken too. Since her husband's death, she's hid the family's money problems from everyone. She's ashamed and doesn't want her kids to worry.

Since his death, she's been selling stuff to pay off their debts and try to deal with it, but there's nothing left. If she can't pay, her sons will be taken as slaves for payment. She's already lost so much and she's afraid to lose even more. She's got nothing left to help those she loves most.

Her grief, desperation, fear, and helplessness push her to Elisha's door. She pours out her story and reminds him that she's a prophet's wife, someone we'd think didn't deserve to go through this. Elisha hears all of this and says, "How can I help you?" and before she can answer adds, "Tell me, what do you have in your house?" (v. 2).

Her response echoes that of the first widow, "Your servant has nothing there at all, except a little oil" (v. 2). But this time, the strategy God uses for a miracle is different. Elisha tells the widow, "Go outside, borrow vessels from all your neighbors, empty vessels and not too few. Then go in and shut the door behind yourself and your sons and pour into all these vessels. And when one is full, set it aside" (v. 3-4).

She probably tells her boys something like, "Mommy needs your help with something. Go around to the neighbors' houses and ask them if they have any empty jars that we can have. Don't forget to say please!" When she feels like she has nothing left to give, she has to learn to rest in the helping hands of others rather than push them away because she feels unworthy.

When she's collected as many jars as she can, she closes the door behind her and her boys. Just like with the Shunammite woman's son and Jairus' daughter, this miracle wasn't for everyone. It was for her and her sons first. Her son hands her the first bottle, and she pours. Another bottle, and it's still working!

They start moving faster and getting more and more excited as the oil just keeps pouring. When there are no more jars to fill, the oil finally stops flowing. She runs to tell Elisha, and he says, "Go, sell the oil and pay off your debts. You and your sons can live on what is left" (v. 7).

This was obviously to get the creditors off her back, but it is also a witness to the community. It likely provides for some other struggling families. And it tests her faith again because she can't keep her whole stockpile for herself.

Emptiness can make you aware of your loneliness. It can make you feel lost, like you have nothing to contribute, like you don't have enough to even make it. If you try to find people to fill that loneliness, you'll only be disappointed, and it won't be their fault.

It is an emptiness only filled by God. When we feel empty, we need to cry out to God. We can't pretend it's all okay. We can't fill up our lives with busyness trying to fill the emptiness. After we cry out to God, we have to reach out to others. This isn't blasting our personal lives on Facebook, but it also isn't saying, "it's none of your business" to everyone who cares for us. You don't have to share everything with everyone, but you do have to share something with someone.

> There comes a point in the healing process for all of us where we have to close the door and let God pour.

We need people who will help us bring our empty things to the table so God can fill them. When we're desperate to heal ourselves for the sake of those we love but don't know how, we need people who will share their emptiness too. Sometimes you'll be the one asking for jars, and sometimes you'll be the one giving them away. But only the empty jars that are given to God will get poured into.

There comes a point in the healing process for all of us where we have to close the door and let God pour. You can have your privacy, but there are some people in your life you can't hide from. For this woman, it was her kids.

They had to be a part of the pouring. What feels like weakness to us, looks like strength to those in our lives. In her weakest moment, she was building her sons' faith.

She was in survival mode, which makes us hoard everything: money, time, emotions, stuff. But Elisha had told her to pour. As she poured, her not enough turned into overflow.

God didn't just give her enough to pay off her debts. He gave her more than enough so she had extra to live on. He took the weight off her shoulders that said she had to do everything for her family. And he even gave her enough to bless others. It wasn't a pity gift; it was a promise of His provision.

Sometimes pouring feels like a sacrifice no one else will ever see, but God sees and HE will pour into us until we overflow (Luke 6:38). While we're pouring, we experience His grace, love, joy, and provision. But if we wait until we're full to pour, we'll never experience the power of God in our lives.

Holly Furtick says, "Don't be afraid of the empty spaces because empty is where God does His best work."5 God will turn our empty desperation into overflowing provision if we trust Him enough to pour a little. Pour even if you're still whole*ish*.

<u>Fill the Holes:</u>

- What do you have in your life that you've written off as nothing? Could it be that this is the very thing God wants to use for a miracle?

- Do you think the widow's oil would have kept flowing if she'd gotten more empty jars? How many are you willing to bring Him? (The more emptiness we're willing to hand over, the more He can fill.)

- When you cry out to God, the first thing He wants to work on is YOU. What is God trying to change within you so that He can use you to pour into others?

<u>Prayer:</u> *Jesus, neither of these women are named in Scripture, and yet you know them by name. You did miracles in their lives we're still talking about. You know all my empty places, all the areas I feel not enough. I pray You'd give me the faith to lay my emptiness out on the table and trust You to fill it. Don't let me go looking for someone or something else to fill what only You can. Don't let me hide my emptiness out of shame. Don't let my pride keep me from asking others for help. Instead, fill me up*

pour by pour. Use my overflow to pour into others, like these women's stories have poured into me. You are faithful to protect and provide for me down to the very last drop. Thank You, Jesus, for not leaving me to do that on my own.

CHAPTER 14:

MESSY AND MIRACULOUS

RESTORATION

John 9:1-41; Mark 8:22-26 [1]

After avoiding stoning by a mob, Jesus passes by a man who was born blind. His disciples immediately ask whose fault it is that this poor guy was born blind. Why do we always try to find someone or something to blame when things don't meet our expectations?

Jesus tells them it's no one's fault, "but this happened so that the work of God might be displayed in him" (John 9:3). His "defect" or "deficiency" is not to punish him, but so God's power might be displayed in his life.

The passage doesn't say the man asks for help or healing. Maybe he doesn't recognize Jesus' voice, and he obviously can't see him. Maybe he has just given up on ever being healed. But Jesus hasn't given up on his healing.

He bends down to the ground, spits in the dirt, and makes some mud. Was he spitting in disgust at him? Was he getting some junk out of his throat? What was he doing? He picked up the mud and caked it onto the man's eyes. No health waiver signed, no permission asked, no plan for the guy to think over. Just mud *on his eyes*!

Jesus says, "Go, wash in the pool of Siloam" (v. 7). He doesn't give excuses, question the directions, gripe about the mud, or decide it's too ridiculous and too much trouble to try again. The man just goes and washes, and comes home seeing. How did he get to the pool though? He had to be willing to ask others for help along the way, and not just Jesus.

Sometimes we need healing from pain, loss, or trauma that is not our fault. We didn't do anything to cause it, but we also can't heal ourselves from it. That's why Jesus is always looking to heal us, even when we don't see it coming, even when we've given up on it, and even when we don't recognize the healing opportunity right in front of us. The man didn't have a clue what Jesus was up to, but he lets him in close anyway.

When he does, Jesus makes things even messier for him. Mud on your eyes is the last thing anyone would think should be there or would help. It's not what you want.

Sometimes God uses what we don't want or what we think will hurt us more in order to heal us. Sometimes it's the last thing we expect that leads to our miracle.

Healing isn't a comfortable process. Healing isn't usually a neat and tidy process either. Think about every image you've ever seen of an operating room. There's blood and gauze everywhere, and surgery recovery is painful.

Just like with the mud, things are going to get messy in our healing process. Some translations say Jesus, "anointed his eyes" with the mud. We don't think rubbing mud on anyone's eyes could be anointed. It might be considered assault. But with Jesus, even when it's messy, every touch in our lives is anointed.

> **Sometimes it's the last thing we expect that leads to our miracle.**

When the man comes back to town, seeing for the first time, he gets mixed responses. Some people believe he really is the same blind man they saw begging before. But others aren't buying it. Even when he tells them the whole story, the religious leaders just ask where this "Jesus" is he claims healed him.

Some people in your life will accept the new you Jesus has transformed because they wanted you to be whole all along, and others will push you away because their codependency isn't needed anymore.

As the man continues to proclaim what Jesus did to the crowd of haters at the synagogue, he tells them, "If this man was not from God, he could do nothing" (v. 33). This is a man who never met Jesus prior to his healing. He's fully convinced that if Jesus wasn't God, his healing wouldn't even have been possible. The same is true for us. If it's down to ourselves or only human power, our deepest healing will never be possible.

When the religious get tired of hearing his story and cast him out, Jesus finds him. He asks the man, "Do you believe in the Son of Man?" (v. 35). and then explains that He, Jesus, is that Son of Man—the messiah. The man believes in him and receives a whole other level of healing.

Jesus didn't leave him with just physical healing, which is the part we usually focus on. He made sure he was spiritually healed and whole too. He helped him see physically and then see spiritually. In life, spiritually blind people will always be beggars until they can see who they are—worthy and whole in Christ.

Jesus didn't heal this man's money problems, societal problems, or relational problems. He fixed the deeper issue causing those problems: a vision problem. The biggest proof of his transformation is that he repeatedly shares his story instead of begging on the sidelines. We have to decide in our own lives if we want Jesus to *heal* us or just give us relief.

🔃🔃🔃

Have you ever had someone in your life you wished you could help, but didn't know how? Odds are you probably have. In Mark 8 there are some unnamed heroes who see a blind man and decide to do what they can to help him. We don't know how they knew him or why they cared so much, but thankfully they did.

You don't see these people trying to give the guy some cream for his eyes or tell him what to try because it's not their responsibility to heal him. It is just their responsibility to get him to the One who can. So they bring him to Jesus and "beg Jesus to touch him" (Mark 8:22). Jesus takes the man by the hand and leads him outside the village.

The man is probably expecting Jesus to say or do something special to heal him, but then he hears that nasty hacking sound. Jesus skips the mud this time and spits *on* the man's eyes. Then he puts his hands on them and asks if he sees anything.

The man squints for a second and says, "I see people; they look like trees walking around" (v. 24). So "once more Jesus puts his hands on the man's eyes. Then his eyes are opened, and his sight is restored, and he sees everything clearly" (v. 25). Jesus sends him home with directions not to go into the village they just left. A little walk, a little spit, and suddenly a man can see. This story left me with so many questions at first.

Why did this blind man let Jesus lead him outside the city? Living blind is extremely vulnerable. I wonder how many people had lied to him before and led him into places he didn't want to be in or told him things that weren't true. When you live with no vision, you are susceptible to the misleading voices around you.

But vulnerability isn't a weakness. This man's miracle started when he was willing to trust someone in his life to lead him to Jesus and then let Jesus lead him somewhere unfamiliar. Robert Madu says, "Victory isn't just found in your valor. It's found in your vulnerability."[2]

> ...you'll only be able to connect when you get vulnerable.

In your own life, you may be able to lead with your strength, and there's nothing wrong with that. But you'll only be able to connect when you get vulnerable. Jesus is the perfect example of both.

Why did the people who brought the man to Jesus not ask him to heal him? They just said touch him. I think they knew just one touch from Jesus would change everything. And that's exactly what it did.

Touch has a huge impact on our emotions and therefore our whole lives. There's a reason they're called "feelings." Our realities are composed of what our senses tell us about the world around us. When Jesus touches him, his whole reality changes.

This man was able to see at some earlier point earlier in his life, or else he would have no idea what trees look like. We don't know how or when he lost his sight, but he lived with this part of himself shut off for a while.

When Jesus restores his sight, he doesn't just make him physically whole. This man is able to fully feel again. He can see the faces of those he loves, take in a sunrise, or watch the world around him. One touch from Jesus will change your whole reality.

Why did Jesus spit again? What's his deal with spit? He's not mean, rude, or disgusting. In fact, in that culture they understood spit to have medicinal purposes. He knew the real healing was in his hands, but he was willing to meet the man where he was. It was an act of compassion.

When Jesus' first move was to touch his hand, not his eyes, he was probably a little confused. His hand wasn't the problem. But he let Jesus lead him, farther and farther down the road. That's what faith looks like. You don't have to know everything or be perfect to find healing. You just have to be willing to be led. The willing ones are the ones who get healed.

Why did Jesus lead him out of the village? Couldn't he have just spit in his eyes where they were? Matthew 11:20-21 explains that Jesus knew this village was a place of unbelief. He did lots of miracles there, only for people to still doubt and criticize, and he didn't want that to ruin this man's vision.

We have to make sure our village isn't ruining our vision too. Going to church on Sunday is a great thing, but if those you're around Monday to Saturday are clouding things up for you with fear, doubt, shame, pain, or worry, it's time to get a new village.

Last question: why didn't the man see clearly on the first try? Jesus obviously could have done it that way. It wasn't a lack of power. He did lots of miracles where he simply spoke and people were healed! I think he wanted to see if the man would be honest about his current condition.

God doesn't need your perfection, but He does need your honesty. He is a God that will move you from blind to blurry.[3] Blurry might be slightly better than blind, but we hate uncertainty! We want things to change so we can see immediately. However, sometimes the blurriness serves a purpose.

When things are blurry, you have to get close to Jesus for clarity. Don't give up when life's blurry. Don't give up when your first step toward healing doesn't heal everything. It's hard to be honest when it's blurry, but if you aren't, you may not get to clarity. Don't walk away after the first touch.

> God doesn't need your perfection, but He does need your honesty.

Let God keep working to heal you until things are clear and whole again. No matter what you've lost, God is a God of restoration.

Scars take anywhere from twenty-one days to two years to fully form after we're wounded.[4] With Jesus' crucifixion, his wounds were scars in three days. That's proof of how healing works with Jesus. He can take the trauma the world says will take forever for you to heal from and restore you far sooner with His love.

You've been wounded long enough. Why choose to stay that way when healing is in His hands? Your loved ones don't need you to be perfect or cover up your wounds. They just need you to be honest when things are hurting and willing to keep walking through the messy process of healing.

Don't stay blind because you're afraid of the mud. Dive into the mess of healing. Let Him show you how to see clearly again.

Fill the Holes:

- What are you angry about in your life that isn't your fault? Where do you feel like you've failed or lacked? How can you start seeing that area of your life as a place where Jesus' power can be demonstrated?

- Is there a part of yourself you've lost that's keeping you from being able to fully feel and engage the world around you? Are you willing to let Jesus heal that part of you if it requires you to be vulnerable?

- The pool the first man was sent to, Siloam, means "sent." Will you go wherever and to whomever He sends you for healing? Will you do whatever He asks you to do to heal?

Prayer: *Jesus, I feel helpless to fix some parts of myself and parts of my life. Some of the pain I didn't cause, and I know that. But it still hurts. Things are blurry, and I don't know what to do. I feel like I've lost a part of myself I'll never get back. Jesus, please touch my life. Touch my heart, with the very hands that were wounded to set me free. Heal me fully and give me back my vision. Restore broken places in my family, broken relationships in my life, and broken situations around me. You are all powerful. No wound is too big for you to mend. Give me strength to be vulnerable in this messy process. I don't want to stop until I'm whole.*

CHAPTER 15:
LOVE COVERS IT ALL

Hosea 1-14 [1]

What if the part of you that's broken is your ability to love and receive love? What if you feel like you're missing that chunk of your heart due to something in the past? How can you possibly heal from that, right?

Maybe you've heard of broken heart syndrome (or takotsubo cardiomyopathy) before. If you're like me, you thought for the longest time that it couldn't possibly be a real thing, but it turns out it is! It's a condition where the left ventricle of your heart is reshaped into something that resembles an octopus trap (thus the Japanese name "takotsubo").[2] The ventricle is larger in size with a more narrow neck, which doesn't let blood flow properly.

Grief and trauma are leading causes. They literally reshape our hearts. In a metaphorical sense, when our hearts are broken we have a harder time giving and receiving what we need most.

Hosea's story occurs in a time where God's people have lost all hope that He can redeem them. They've been unfaithful and failed so many times they don't see a way out. Their hearts are broken, and God chooses to use Hosea's life as a dramatic demonstration.

The first thing God tells Hosea to do is go take "a wife of whoredom," a.k.a. a prostitute, and have children with her. We don't know much about Hosea, but I picture him as a pretty straight-laced, genuinely kind, overall good guy. If I'm Hosea and God tells me to go marry someone I don't know, who may not even want to marry me, and who has obviously had a rough life, I'm going to have some questions at the very least!

> ...when our hearts are broken we have a harder time giving and receiving what we need most.

But not Hosea. The next three words after God tells him who to marry are, "so he went" (1:3). He must have trusted that what God told him to do would ultimately be for his good and God's glory. He wasn't focused on whether this was fair or what he was "owed" for being a good guy. He just went and married a prostitute named Gomer.

Hosea and Gomer's first three children's names give insight to the estrangement between God and Israel. They mean things like, "not loved" and "not my people." But that wasn't the end of God's love for them or His plan to redeem them. He says, "I will bring her [Israel] into the wilderness, and speak tenderly to her. There I will give her back her vineyards and make the Valley of Achor [trouble] a door of hope" (2:14-15).

Because the people of Israel went off looking for love in all the wrong places, God brings them to the wilderness. That's not a fun place, but it's where He's able to get close enough to get their attention again and speak to them. He wants to turn their "valley of trouble," their low and dark place, into a door of hope. But here's the thing about doors; you have to choose whether to walk through them or turn around and walk away.

I can't imagine the trauma Gomer went through. It's easier for most of us to judge her than try to walk in her shoes for a minute and think about what she's seen, what she's endured, and what she's been forced to accept. It must have been painful to feel used, unworthy, and have a dollar amount determine your value.

You might think it makes no sense for someone from her background to leave a stable, good man like Hosea. But that's exactly what she does. One day she just walks away from him and their children. People responding from a place of trauma can push away stable relationships because they don't know how to live in anything that's not chaos. They may not know how to accept unconditional love because their experience tells them it must be earned or deserved.

Trauma and fear, no matter the cause, can rewire us so that we're afraid to trust the good, afraid to even open a gift, afraid to believe someone really does have our best interests at heart. That way of life can be just as damaging as the traumatic event itself.

> Trauma and fear, no matter the cause, can rewire us so that we're afraid to trust the good, afraid to even open a gift, afraid to believe someone really does have our best interests at heart.

As this mom lives on the streets again, selling her body for money, she's never felt more self-loathing, shame, or regret. She misses those three kids she's left at home and longs for Hosea's embrace. She's fighting just to keep her head above water, and as long as that's the case, she won't be able to fight for connection with someone else.

But remember, their marriage is to be a picture of God's love for His people. He promised Israel, "I will betroth you to me forever. I will betroth you to me in righteousness and in justice, in steadfast love and in mercy. I will betroth you to me in faithfulness" (2:19-20). God's love wasn't done, so neither was Hosea's.

God tells him, "Go, show your love to your wife again, though she is loved by another and is an adulteress. Love her as the Lord loves the Israelites" (3:1). I know 1 Corinthians 13 says, "love never ends," but Hosea is probably wondering right now if that's a beautiful promise or a nagging weight.

How brutal this must be for Hosea. He's still got three kids at home who've endured so much. He's experienced his own trauma in this saga too. Watching someone push you away out of trauma response is like watching an addict drink themselves to death. You feel helpless and hurt for them, but all the while they're hurting you too. Still, God says it's time, so Hosea clings to that promise he made to Gomer and God and goes to get her.

If someone tells you, "nobody likes messy," I call bull! From an early age, we find joy in making messes. Kids draw all over the walls, splash bubbles out of the bathtub, and have no problem dumping a whole pile of blocks onto the floor. But as we grow up, we're taught to put away the mess or not to make it in the first place.

Believe me, I understand the value in that and I am not a proponent of clutter, poor hygiene, or people who can't clean up after themselves. Anyone who knows me knows I'm an organized and neat person, sometimes to an extent others laugh at! It's in my DNA. However, I think there has to be space to dump out our mess.

Even the clean freak in me finds joy in making a mess sometimes, like when I paint or sort through a whole closet of junk. We have to find people in our lives who aren't afraid of our messes, but who in fact are willing to sit down in the pile with us, laugh or cry about the whole thing, and then help us find some order in the mess.

If the person who loves you says, "show me your messiest closet and let's do this," don't run out of the room because you don't want them to see it. That just leaves you alone and with an even bigger mess to deal with.

Let love into your mess. Love isn't as warm and fuzzy as you may have made it out to be. Love means putting on gloves and diving into the mess until the mess becomes freedom, joy, and beauty again.

🔁🔁🔁

When Hosea finds Gomer, she's become someone else's property. He has to buy her back for six ounces of silver before she can even come home with him. I imagine that walk home was a tense one, with Gomer's eyes staring straight at the ground. She's spent all this time away from home beating herself up in her own head.

> Let love into your mess.

Author and speaker Lisa Harper says, "the words of death the enemy speaks usually match the bruises in our hearts."[3] Whispers of shame like, "You know this is all you ever deserved." Whispers of doubt like, "You know Hosea never really loved you." And whispers of fear like, "What if you die like this and never see your kids again?"

When we let trauma scar us, it shapes our perspective. Everything in life starts to seem like a personal attack in our minds. Pastor of Union Church, Stephen Chandler, says, "Because of this warped perspective, we see our one-time trauma as a life-long sentence."[4] Scientists explain that trauma can affect our beliefs about the future due to a loss of hope, limit our expectations about life, make us fear that life will end abruptly or early, or lead us to anticipate that normal life events won't occur.[5] It can lead to numbing and avoiding all possible triggers of the traumatic event as much as possible.[6]

Trauma only begets more trauma until healing breaks the cycle.

God connects the dots for Israel when He says, "You walk away from your God at the drop of a hat and like a whore sell yourself promiscuously... You'll end up hungrier than ever... bankrupt... disillusioned... and your souls polluted by the spirit—dirty air. You'll be starved for God, exiled from God's own country" (9:1-6).

> **Trauma only begets more trauma until healing breaks the cycle.**

This is how it feels when we *try* to walk away from God's love—hungry for more, running out of what we need, confused, starving for something real, alone, and with a heart that's polluted by darkness. "You have abandoned the love you had at first. Remember therefore from where you have fallen;

repent, and do the works you did at first" (Rev 2:4-5,ESV). Those descriptions may sound harsh, but they're true.

Some of us are living in cold marriages. Some are too paralyzed by fear to even look for love for fear of being rejected or losing it again. The good news is, that's not the kind of love we were intended to have. To get to the real stuff, we have to know God's love for us intimately. His love doesn't ignore our failures or let us sit in shame. It seeks repentance and restoration.

For us to love well, we have to let Him work in us. Love at work is 1 Corinthians 13 in motion: being patient (even with ourselves), trusting, forgiving, hoping again. But how do you love like you've never been hurt before? How do you risk something like you've never failed before?

Christ has to take our old things and make them new (2 Cor. 5:17). He has to rework our muscle memory until we stop running on autopilot and turning back to our old shame, fear, and pain. That's not something we can do ourselves. "You thought you could do it all on your own, flush with weapons and manpower. But the volcano of war will erupt among your people. All your defense posts will be leveled" (Hosea 10:11-15).

If we think we deal with all our issues on our own, it will only lead to war within us and with those around us. All the walls we put up as defenses in attempts to prove we're all good will eventually come down one way or another. It may be in a voluntary remodeling or an unexpected fire, but there's no wall we can put up that can keep out God's love for us.

Love is a fight, not because you should be with someone you always fight with. No, the fight is to pursue the other person recklessly, like Hosea pursued Gomer, like God pursues us. The fight is also within yourself, to not let your own shame, pain, and fear put up walls that keep you locked away from others' love.

That was Gomer's battle and is ours if we're going to accept God's love for us. We have to stop thinking God's hired us. The truth is He's adopted us! His love is not something we work to keep or could ever earn. It's free no matter what.

"What are you waiting for? Return to your God! Commit yourself in love, in justice. Wait for your God, and don't give up on him—ever!" (12:6). God will "heal your waywardness and love you freely" (14:4). This messy but beautiful story is a crystal clear picture of God's love that redeems us, a love that reaches us in our lowest place.

It will walk through any wall, conquer any shame, and overcome any doubt. Only His love is deep enough and big enough to cover all of our brokenness and make us whole.

Fill the Holes:

- God told Hosea to do something so that He could speak through his life. What God tells us to do isn't just about us. Are you available for God to speak to you so that He can use you? Are you willing to let Him transform your trauma into a testimony of His love?

- It's easy to picture yourself as Hosea in the story, but how are you like Gomer? Have you let your pain lead you to dark places you're already free from?

- What are you believing about love (what it looks like, your ability to give or receive it, or even God's love for you) that you need to let God reshape and rework?

Prayer: *God, I know you made me for love. It's hardwired into my soul. And yet we as humans fail at it daily. It's such a messy thing to love and be loved, especially when my heart is warped by pain and loss. But that's why I need Your perfect love. Even when I run out of shame, You pursue me. Even when I put up walls out of fear, You knock them down. You stop at nothing to restore my heart and make me whole. Your love "bears all things, believes all things, hopes all things, endures all things. It never ends" (1 Cor. 13:7-8). Teach me to trust Your love for me. Show me how to love like You love me, even when it's messy.*

CHAPTER 16:

NEVER TOO HARD TO

HEAL

Acts 9:1-22, 16:16-40, 26:12-29, 27, 28 [1]

"Saul was still breathing threats and murder" (9:1). That's the start of a sinister thriller if I've ever heard one.

If up to this chapter you've been thinking to yourself, "Yea, that's a nice story and I'm glad it worked out for them. But my heart is too hard to heal. I'm too broken to be 'whole' again," then this is the chapter for you.

Saul is beyond your average "bad guy." There's something so broken in him that he's made it his life mission to destroy and kill every Christian he can find and he tells himself he's doing something holy while he's doing it! But as hard as it may be to believe, this same mouth that's breathing violence will soon be spilling the Gospel to thousands of people. There's just a hard heart to heal first.

Saul decides Damascus is his next city on the hit list. He asks the priest for access to the synagogues to check and see if he can find any Christians to take as prisoners. (So messed up that the priest gave him permission!) And he heads into town.

That's when "a light from heaven flashes around him," and he falls to the ground (9:3-4). He hears a voice say, "'Saul, Saul, why do you persecute me?' 'Who are you, Lord?' Saul asks. 'I am Jesus, whom you are persecuting. Now get up and stand on your feet... I am sending you to open [the Gentiles'] eyes and turn them from darkness to light, and from the power of Satan to God, so that they may receive forgiveness of sins and a place among those who are sanctified by faith in me'" (26:15-18).

That's a quick turn of events! The man who was just talking smack about killing Christians and telling the priests he was going to their synagogues on a manhunt is now on his knees, blind, and has to be led into a city for instructions he hasn't even been given yet.

Encountering Jesus can be humbling, unexpected, and even confusing sometimes. It certainly was for Saul. Yet, we don't see Jesus punish him, even though most of us would say it was deserved. Nor does he leave Saul alone and blind in a timeout to figure out what he's done wrong. Jesus actually provides for him in this transformation, without his knowledge.

While Saul is slowly being led into Damascus by his men (who aren't Christians, yet God uses anyway), the Lord appears to a man in Damascus named Ananias. In a vision, the Lord tells him in so many words, "I'm sending you to the murderer, Saul, so you can heal his blindness. Ok? Cool".

Ananias is not cool with it at first and starts to rattle off all the horrible stuff he's heard about Saul. Jesus doesn't say anything about what Saul has done or even acknowledge Ananias' fears about Saul killing him. He just says, "Go, for he is a chosen instrument of *mine* to carry my name..." (9:15).

There's nothing to suggest Ananias has laid hands on anyone before to heal them. He's listening to Jesus and willing to trust He can use him for big things, even scary things. Thankfully for Saul and the future of the entire Church, he decides that God's power to change Saul's heart is greater than Saul's power to bind up believers.

Ananias goes to the house where he was told Saul would be and knocks on the door. When it opens, he finds Saul praying. Yep, praying! His encounter with the light of God has led him to fall on his knees. That's exactly what we need to do when we question our lives, feel ashamed, or think we've failed beyond repair—hit our knees in prayer.

Saul's desperately praying to see again, and in walks Ananias. He lays his hands on Saul's eyes and says, "Brother Saul, the Lord-Jesus, who appeared to you on the road as you were coming here has sent me so that you may see again and be filled with the Holy Spirit" (9:17).

Immediately Saul's sight is fully restored. But better than the physical healing is the fact that he is given God's Spirit to see the world through God's eyes. His trip to Damascus looked nothing like he planned, but God turned Saul's plan all around to set him free.

He is baptized, a sign of his old life passing away and new life coming in. Then he eats some food and hits the streets. "At once he begins proclaiming Jesus in the synagogues, saying 'He is the Son of God'" (9:20). His transformation results in immediate action, but this was only the start of his transformation. Would it last? Would he continue to hold to the truth of Jesus when he faced pain like what he'd been causing others?

Well, if we check in on Saul years later as he stands in front of King Agrippa, we'll find out. Saul, now named Paul, says, "To this day I have had the help that comes from God, and so I stand here testifying both to small and great" (26:22). He knows that his day to day transformation has only come from God's steady help, and as he looks back he can see how God has worked in big and small ways.

No matter where we are in our journey, we need God's help in our hoping, healing, and becoming whole.

Saul "increased in strength and confounded the Jews... by proving that Jesus was the Christ" (9:22). How did he prove that? His life change was the proof. Saul tried to bind up the work of God by persecuting Christians, but instead God turned around and set him free.

His life became an example of darkness turning to light and the power of God's grace. Grace turns our mistakes into fuel for a purpose, not fuel for our shame. God's purposes for us supersede the pain we've caused, the failures we've had, and the shame we hide.

> No matter where we are in our journey, we need God's help in our hoping, healing, and becoming whole.

Steven Furtick says, "You can tell yourself a summary of what you are and what you're not based on the experiences that you've had, not the potential that you carry... [But] if we condemn ourselves, we don't have to change."[2] If Paul sat condemning himself for all the pain he caused he wouldn't have needed to change, but he also wouldn't have been used by God.

An encounter with God doesn't lead to shame. It leads to change. So make peace with your past, but don't make peace with your problem. If you do, you'll say, "it's just who I am," accept that you *are* the problem, and

> ...make peace with your past, but don't make peace with your problem.

it'll become part of your identity (see Rom. 7:15,17). Paul, like all of us, admits to still doing things he doesn't want to do.

He's made peace with his past Saul identity (the former persecutor), but he isn't making peace with his problem areas or sin or patterns of pain. We'll see in other events in his life how God continues to work on his heart.

🁢🁢🁢

Paul's ministry explodes and he becomes a traveling church planter and evangelist. One day Paul, and his friend, Silas, are on their way to the temple when they're stopped by a slave girl who's demon-possessed. She's been making her master's money by telling people's futures.

For days she follows Paul and Silas around and keeps saying, "These men are servants of the Most High God" (16:17). She's not wrong, but Paul gets irritated and casts the demon out of her. You'd think that's a good thing for this poor girl, but her masters are furious! Their money-making scheme is over.

They grab Paul and Silas and take them to the local court (of sorts). That's when things get really nasty.

The crowd turns against them, makes up lies about them, strips and beats them, and then throws them in prison. Now Paul sits where he used to throw Christians, himself. They don't deserve this. We'd expect them to be bitter, angry, disappointed with God and the people, or at the very least tired of doing the right thing, only to get blindsided. I would have felt all those things! Not Paul and Silas.

"About midnight Paul and Silas are praying and singing hymns to God" (16:25). That's not the sign of men who are bitter or angry or blaming God. It's also not the sign of men who believe "I deserve this because of all the persecuting I used to do." It's a sign of their surrender to God's will and their healed hearts. They know God is sovereign over the screw-ups of people.

While they're singing, "there is a great earthquake" that shakes the prison down to its foundation. "Immediately all the doors are opened, and everyone's bonds are unfastened" (16:26). I'm sure there is some hooping and hollering from all the prisoners when their chains fall off. But the jailor flips out.

If the prisoners turn on him, he's dead. If the authorities find out he's lost all the prisoners, he's dead. So he goes to take his own life, but Paul yells, "Don't harm yourself! We're all here!" (16:28). Notice he doesn't yell, "Boom! I told you my God was big enough to get me out of your stupid prison. Peace out man!" That's probably what I'd want to say.

But this is another sign of the healing that God's done in Paul's heart. He takes what could have easily been an opportunity for revenge and sees it as an opportunity for redemption. When our sole focus stops being revenge or our selfish idea of justice, that's evidence of God's healing in our hearts. You can't see beyond those things with a hard heart.

Not only does God set them free, but he has their jailor bind up their wounds at his own house. The jailor ends up believing in Christ and before it's all over, the policeman who wrongfully imprisoned them comes to them personally and apologizes before telling them to go free. God moves in their darkest moment (literally midnight) to set them free.

But it wasn't just about their freedom. He frees the other prisoners physically and frees the jailor spiritually. Only God's handiwork can do something like this. He healed Paul's heart so he can use him in this painful situation. Then he uses the painful situation to heal others with hard hearts.

> God moves in their darkest moment (literally midnight) to set them free.

As Paul goes about his ministry he faces tons of obstacles and unfair treatment from wrongful imprisonment to beatings to starvation (see 2 Cor. 11:23-28). Yet, God must have truly healed his heart because he never appears to carry bitterness or resentment about it.

⌘⌘⌘

One of the many things Paul endures is a brutal shipwreck.

He's being shipped to Rome as a prisoner to face trial. This requires quite a boat ride from one side of the Mediterranean Sea to the other. After multiple boat transfers and a long journey, they still aren't there and winter is approaching.

Paul tries to warn them, saying, "Men, I can see that our voyage is going to be disastrous and bring great loss to ship and cargo, and to our own lives also" (27:10). In true stubborn fashion, no one wants to listen to him, and they sail on anyway. After multiple days of battering winds, missing the island they were hoping for, and throwing everything overboard, they end up stuck in the shallow waters with their anchor down getting smacked around by relentless storms.

We do this too. We ignore God's direction and decide we're just going to muscle through to wherever we think we need to go, but then the shallow things hang us up and we get stuck somewhere we weren't ever supposed to be.

"All hope of being saved is abandoned," and Paul chimes in with a solid, "I told you so". I'd be saying at least that much! But he also tells them an angel has appeared to him and promised, "Do not be afraid, Paul; you must stand before Caesar. And behold, God has granted you all those who sail with you". He tells them, "Take heart, men, for I have faith in God that it will be exactly as I have been told" (27:23-25).

I'm sure that didn't immediately calm everyone's fears, but Paul was confident that even though man had screwed up, even though they were in the middle of a storm, and even though it didn't look like what they planned, God was still in charge and would get them where He promised. God's favor is waiting for them in the place their mistakes would land them.

After fourteen nights of floating around in the dark storms, they sense that they're getting close to land only to run into a sandbar. The boat shatters into pieces and they all have to swim or float to shore on pieces of the boat. On the island called Malta they find very hospitable people who help them make a fire to get warm in the rainy, cold weather.

Paul, trying to be a team player, throws some wood onto the fire and a viper latches onto his hand! As the islanders watch this unfold, no one tries to help him. They just throw blame, saying it must mean he's a murderer and deserves to die. We have a tendency when bad things happen to want to point the finger. But there's never been any power released from a pointing finger.

The crazy part is they're not wrong. Paul *was* a murderer. But if Paul accepts the identity they've given him at this moment, he dies. Instead of stopping to think about whether he deserves this or not, he just shakes the snake off. Take that Bear Grylls!

This demonstrates how healed of his shame he is by this point or he might have agreed that it was his fault somehow. If we hold onto what's hurting us, the shame, the lies, the blame... it will penetrate our identity. We'll start asking things like, "What's wrong with me? Why doesn't anyone want to be around me?" That's not God.

How easy would it have been for Paul to think God was punishing him for all he'd done in his early life? The fact that he doesn't is evidence of God's transformation and grace.

The islanders, like us, are fickle people, and decide since Paul doesn't get sick or die from the snake bite that he must be a god. That gets him an invite to meet the chief official, Publius. It turns out that Publius has a father who is sick with a fever and diarrhea (yikes!).

> Some of our biggest mistakes come from holding onto the wrong thing too much and not holding onto the right thing enough.

Paul goes in to check on him. After praying, he "places his hands on him and heals him" (28:9). His wounded hand was used to heal someone else because he didn't hold onto the pain. If Paul was too busy blaming the people of the island, he would've missed what God wanted to do on the island while he was there.[3]

You can point your finger at God when you need to. He's not scared of it, but it won't heal you. You can point to your past, but it won't heal you either. You can point to things that can't point back, like the government, but it won't heal you. In our relationships, pointing fingers actually kills communication, empathy, and connection. Only open hands allow healing.

Some of our biggest mistakes come from holding onto the wrong thing too much and not holding onto the right thing enough. Like that snake, we hold onto our hurt by being defensive instead of holding onto our relationships with those we love. We hold onto the accusations we've made against ourselves for so long instead of holding onto God's grace. We hold onto our shame instead of holding onto the freedom we have in Christ.

Take your hand that's been hurt and lay it in God's. His hands have always been open to you. And His hands will make you whole.

Paul went from pointing fingers at Christians to throwing them in prison to extending hands of healing because *he* received healing. Paul suffered a great deal, and yet he loved others, preached freedom even while in chains, had joy, persisted in faith, and walked humbly with God. If that's not evidence that God can heal the hardest of hearts, I don't know what is.

Fill the Holes:

- Do you believe the severity of your situation or the extent of your fear is more powerful than God's power to change it? Do you believe your heart is harder than God's love can reach? Or do you believe God's plan for healing is more powerful than it all?

- God's hand has always been open to you, but is your hand open to Him? Or are you holding onto something that's keeping you from healing?

- If you had to pinpoint the hardest part of your heart, the part you try not to think about and don't want to talk about, what would it be? Are you ready to let God soften it? He wants to take the hardest heart and turn it into one that brings healing to others.

Prayer: *Jesus, there are hard parts of my heart that I've just let callus over the years. Places that have been brutally hurt by others, painful memories I don't want to face, and mistakes I'd rather not own. And yet, all that means is that I'm holding onto things that are killing me. I can't do this anymore. I'm opening my hand and my heart. I need You to soften my heart again. Help me to forgive (even myself). Help me to grieve in a healthy way that allows me to move on. Help my wounds to heal. Grant me certainty in chaos, strength in weakness, and healing in snake-bitten hands.*

CHAPTER 17:

HEALING IN THE RAIN

Ezekiel 37:1-14 [1]

Ezekiel may not be at the top of your Bible reading plan, and there's definitely some confusing and weird stories in it. But in Ezekiel 37, there is a story that I feel serves as a beautiful and powerful metaphor for the healing journey we're on.

The prophet Ezekiel is sent by God to speak to the people of Israel, who have once again gone off the rails. Ezekiel is sent to remind them of God's love for them. One day God's Spirit shows Ezekiel a vision of a deserted valley, a valley full of bones, and God asks, "Can these bones live?" (Ezek. 37:3).

This feels like a trick question. They're already dead. Ezekiel's response is brilliant. He says, "O Sovereign Lord, you alone know" (v. 3). That feels like a solid answer—put it back on God. But then there's a curveball.

God says, "Prophesy to the bones and say to them, 'Dry bones, hear the word of the Lord! This is what the Sovereign Lord says to these bones: I will make breath enter you, and you will come to life. I will attach tendons to you and make flesh come upon you and cover you with skin; I will put breath in you, and you will come to life. Then you will know that I am the Lord" (v. 4-6). If this feels like the start of the creepiest sci-fi movie you've ever seen, stay with me.

We don't get to know what Ezekiel is thinking at this moment. He just "prophesies as he's commanded". As he's speaking over the bones, "there is a noise, a rattling sound, and the bones come together, bone to bone ...tendons and flesh appear on them and skin covers them, but there is no breath in them" (v. 7).

God tells him, "Prophesy to the breath... breathe into these slain, that they may live". Ezekiel again speaks over the bones, and "breath enters them; they come to life and stand up on their feet—a vast army" (v. 9-10).

By now, I'd be freaking out. But remember, this was a vision, a picture for Israel, and God explains exactly what it means. He tells Ezekiel, "these bones are the whole of Israel. They say, 'Our bones are dried up and our hope is gone; we are cut off.' So say to them... 'O my people, I am going to open your graves and bring you up from them; I will bring you back to the land of Israel. Then you, my people, will know that I am the Lord.... I will put my Spirit in you and you will live, and I will settle you in your own land... I the Lord have spoken, and I have done it" (v. 11-14).

Sometimes God brings us into a valley to show us His resurrecting power. We've all got dead, dry bones in our lives... relationships, dreams, opportunities we think are dead. Like Lazarus, maybe God chose not to intervene when we thought he should have. Or like Peter, we believe we've messed things up so much they'll never be put back together. Those things very well may be dead, but what if God is just waiting to resurrect them? What does that mean? What would it take to see that happen?

> **Sometimes God brings us into a valley to show us His resurrecting power.**

Ezekiel doesn't exactly overflow with confidence when God tells him the plan. He's not sure the bones can live again, and tries to put the answer back on God. But ultimately, he's obedient. That obedience is what ushers in the miracle, even if there was only a little faith behind it. Over and over we've seen a little faith go a long way.

The Shunammite woman has just enough faith to bring Elisha to her son, and her son is brought back to life. Gideon has just enough faith to tear down the idols in the cloak of night, and it starts a revolution that frees his people. The woman with the issue of blood has just enough faith to touch Jesus' robe, and she is healed.

Even if all you have is "faith as small as a mustard seed" (Matt. 17:20-21,NIV), will you take one step toward healing? Call that person. Go to that church. Reach out to a counselor. Go through that box of stuff. Write it down. Say it out loud. Whatever it is God's leading you to do, take

> He comes close, and things start to heal. Parts of our lives, parts of ourselves, start to come back to life.

the one drop of faith He's given you, and do it. It might be the start of your miracle.

Miracles like this are scary when they're coming together. Rattling sounds, bones coming together to form bodies, and then those bodies standing up as whole people. That's the original Walking Dead! Lazarus coming out of a cave smelling and looking like a mummy... Creepy! Saul suddenly going blind... Disorienting!

As God starts doing miracles in the dead places of our lives, things begin to move and shift. That can be scary because we like control. We like comfort. We don't like change. But then He breathes. He comes close, and things start to heal. Parts of our lives, parts of ourselves, start to come back to life.

These bones were supposed to represent "the *whole* of Israel," but there was nothing whole about them. That was until God took the broken pieces and put them back together. Not back together as slightly better looking dead bodies on the ground. He gave them life and made them a great army.

Total weakness is turned to magnificent strength, brokenness is turned to complete wholeness. The Israelites felt dead inside, helpless, hopeless, and alone. But God opens up the dead places inside them and brings them back to life.

He gives them "a new heart and puts a new spirit within them; He removes their heart of stone and gives them a heart of flesh" (36:26). He gives them hope again and a new home. That's what I pray He does for myself and every reader of this book. If God spoke it, He will do it, just like He did for Israel. Lisa Harper says, "Don't settle for mediocre instead of a miracle...God can resurrect miracles we let die."[2]

🔁🔁🔁

In October 2015, Death Valley received three inches of rain in five hours. That doesn't sound like much until you realize that Death Valley is one of the hottest and driest places on Earth and only gets about two inches of rain (total) per year!

That three inches of rain triggered what's commonly called a "super bloom" in the spring of 2016. Something like this only occurs about once a decade. For years and even decades, millions of seeds stayed buried under the ground, just waiting to bloom. Danny Lewis of the *Smithsonian Magazine* says, "When you get the perfect condition, the perfect storm... those seeds could all sprout at once... Death Valley goes from being a valley of death to being a valley of life."3

Sometimes those dry valleys in our lives and hearts need to experience rain for something to come back to life.

If you're like me, there's a part of you that feels helpless to heal yourself or the ones you love. You feel like those acts of love aren't received, or your attempts to help are dismissed. But every time you reach out anyway it's like a seed planted. It may be planted in dry soil now, but God hasn't forgotten about it. He will send rain in due time.

When things below the cracked surface are dry and dark, we can feel like David did in Psalm 69: weary, exhausted from weeping, and waiting for God to come through for us (Ps. 69:1-3). Then when He sends us rain in the form of a storm, we think we'll drown. It feels like things are breaking apart and washing away. But don't run.

This rain is a blessing. It may not be convenient. It may expose some things we've buried deep. (That may be exactly what's happening as you read this book.) But all the while, it's watering all that's underneath so it can grow. Like Steven Furtick says, "God removes what He needs to remove so He can reveal what He wants to reveal."4 The rain is there to soften us, heal us, and bring forth new things.

"For as the rain and the snow come down from heaven and do not return there but water the earth, making it bring forth and sprout,..so shall my word be that goes out from my mouth; it shall not return empty, but shall accomplish that which I purpose, and shall succeed in the thing for which I sent it" (Isa. 55:6-11,ESV). Let God's word, all these stories we've looked at, wash over you like rain until what's in you comes back to life.

Don't walk around life dehydrated, letting the rain God sends go down the drain of distraction, depression, or doubt. Don't waste it. You've prayed too hard for this and survived too much to not steward this storm.

> **Don't walk around life dehydrated, letting the rain God sends go down the drain of distraction, depression, or doubt.**

A line from Elevation Worship's song "There is a Cloud" reads, "Every seed buried in sorrow God will call forth in its time."[5] Even those tears you've cried over the dead and broken things in your life are watering what's planted in you if they're poured out in prayer. Keep waiting; it won't be wasted. Keep sowing seeds of faith; they will bloom in time. Keep healing when you're only whole*ish*; you will be whole again.

Take heart, take heart, do not be afraid.

The future may be uncertain,

But there is no need to hide away.

Every day is an opportunity to courageously show up,

Even when you do not feel equipped,

Or that you will be enough.

Let grace surprise you,

Setting fire to your bones,

Strengthening your mind,

In the wild of your unknowns.[6]

Morgan Harper Nichols

Fill the Holes:

- Are you willing to let God open up the dead places in your soul to bring new things to life? (Even if it's scary at first?)

- Are you settling for mediocre, just a few blooms every now and then, because you're wasting the rain God's sent you? How can you start to soak it up instead?

- Is there an area of your life or heart that feels more like a grave right now than a garden? (Let God breathe new life into it, and watch what grows!)

<u>Prayer:</u> *Jesus, parts of my soul are like this dry valley full of bones. I've stopped expecting anything to grow there. I've just let the broken pieces sit in piles. But today I feel You breathing new life into those dead places. Put them back together, Lord, and create an even stronger heart in me as You do. Only You know what's buried underneath all the pain, but I pray You'd bring it forth with Your healing rain. I don't want it to stay hidden and locked away. I have hope that there is beauty to be made from these ashes. I trust that You are healing me even now. I will not be broken forever, because You are making me whole.*

CONCLUSION

2 Kings 8:1-6 [1]

I just bought my first house (in the crazy competitive Denver market!), and shortly after moving in, I spent a couple days planting some flowers on my front and back porches. The problem is I planted peony roots (my favorite) and seeds for various flowers, so all the neighbors see right now are pots of dirt sitting out. But I trust that the roots and seeds will bloom *one day*.

That's how crazy we can look when we keep praying and trusting for healing that the world says we should've given up on a long time ago. That's how crazy we sound in our own heads when we take a step toward healing one more time in defiance of the voice nagging that we'll just fail again. But can I take you back to the rest of the story for the Shunammite woman?

Her story picks up again in 2 Kings 8 where she's told by God to leave her home and go ride out a famine in a foreign land for seven years! What? After all she's been through, trusted God for, and seen God do, she's left to "survive" the rest of her life and never see her home again? That's crazy.

But she gets up and goes, like He told her to. When she finally gets to come back, she's lost her home and everything she had. This wasn't what she expected, and it wasn't her fault. "The Lord had called for a famine" (v. 1). But she did have a responsibility.

In the process of surviving, she's lost something. It would have been easy to beat herself up about the things she did while in survival mode, like leave the place she likely buried her husband. In survival mode, some of us give and give so much of ourselves that we become an empty shell and don't know how to receive anymore. Some of us do things to numb the pain just to survive. Some of us are so comfortable in the place we're surviving that we're convinced we'll never see home again. But there comes a time to go home, a time to say "I want it back."

Back in 2 Kings 4, The Shunammite woman pushed away the promise God gave her about having a son in a year, but now she's willing to risk her hope and ask for what she really wants, her home back. She trusts God will provide like He has so many times before and heads to see the king to ask for just that.

While she is on her way, Gehazi (Elisha's former servant who now works for the king) is telling the king stories about all the things he and Elisha saw God do. Right as he gets to the story about the Shunammite woman and her son, he looks up and sees them walking in! He tells the king, "That's her! And that's her son that Elisha brought back to life!" You can always trust God's timing in writing your story.

The boy standing next to her (now more than seven years old) is the son she was too afraid to ask for and then thought she lost. Now he stands here in her time of need to remind her and everyone else that God brought something back to her already. And He was about to do it again.

The king says, "Restore all that was hers, together with all the produce of the fields from the day she left the land until now" (v. 6). God didn't just restore her land to her; He made up for all that she missed out on in the seven years she was away from home. God is the restorer of lost years (Joel 2:25).

"Jehovah Jireh" means "we'll see you do it again." The same God that did that back then, is the God we'll see do it again in this season. The God who helped you survive the famine will bring you back home and restore everything you lost. As Steven Furtick says, "Some of the things you've lost in your life, God won't bring back in the same way. He's going to restore them to you in an even greater way than you've ever seen them before."[2]

In all that time away, she didn't tell herself a story of fear, blame, shame, or disappointment; or the story she told the king would have been very different. Instead, she told the story she knew: the story of God's faithfulness. That's when she got back what she needed.

God always has the last word, and the last word is love. His love never fails, even when we think it's over.

I've thought a thousand times as I write this, "if only I could help you heal, you'd never be broken again." But that's not true. No person will bring you healing but Jesus. The miracle is found in surrendering that idea and both of us laying all our wounds at the feet of the only true Healer.

I want that healing for you with all I have and every word pouring from these pages. But all I have is not enough. All you have is not enough. We are broken pots in the Potter's hands. Those same hands that were wounded for you and me are the hands that will heal us and make us whole. Don't give up hope. God doesn't just create; He recreates. Your story isn't over yet.

*<u>Your Story</u>: The Shunammite woman's story of miraculous resurrection served to restore to her more land than she ever lost and bring her back home. Her story saved her and those she loved, including her son. We never know how our stories of loss, healing, and faith will continue to bless us in later seasons and encourage others in unexpected ways... Like the paralytic man carrying his mat away was a testament to his miraculous healing. Like the widow's jars of oil were testament to her whole community of God's miraculous provision for her broken family... I pray the stories we've looked at from scripture have served as a blessing to you as you read this book. And I pray you won't hesitate to share your own story either.

I invite you to share it on
www.hopinghealingandwholeish.com

I choose to hope for:

_____

I will heal from:

_____

I am going to be whole again.

REFERENCES

Intro

[1] Richman-Abdou, Kelly. "Kintsugi: The Centuries-Old Art of Repairing Broken Pottery with Gold." My Modern Met. Last modified September 5, 2019. Accessed June 29, 2021. *https://mymodernmet.com/kintsugi-kintsukuroi/.*

[2] Ibid.

[3] "The Fractured Beauty of Kintsugi Pottery." Art & Home. Last modified December 3, 2019. *https://artandhome.net/kintsugi-pottery/.*

[4] Scripture quotations are from The Passion Translation®. Copyright © 2017, 2018 by Passion & Fire Ministries, Inc. Used by permission. All rights reserved. ThePassionTranslation.com.

Chapter 1

[1] *The Holy Bible.* New International Version. 1978. *https://www.biblegateway.com.*

[2] *When God Doesn't Make Sense Part 2.* Narrated by Craig Groeschel.

[3] *When God Doesn't Make Sense Part 1.* Narrated by Craig Groeschel.

Chapter 2

[1] *The Holy Bible.* New International Version. 1978. *https://www.biblegateway.com.*

[2] Scripture quotations are from The Passion Translation®. Copyright © 2017, 2018 by Passion & Fire

Ministries, Inc. Used by permission. All rights reserved. ThePassionTranslation.com.

Chapter 3

[1] Scripture quotations are from the ESV® Bible (The Holy Bible, English Standard Version®), copyright © 2001 by Crossway, a publishing ministry of Good News Publishers. Used by permission. All rights reserved.

[2] Ibid.

[3] *Trust Me I'm Trying!* Narrated by Steven Furtick.

[4] *Trapped in Transition.* Narrated by Steven Furtick.

[5] *The Frustration of Expectation.* Narrated by Rich Wilkerson, Jr.

Chapter 4

[1] Scripture quotations are from the ESV® Bible (The Holy Bible, English Standard Version®), copyright © 2001 by Crossway, a publishing ministry of Good News Publishers. Used by permission. All rights reserved.

[2] Ibid.

[3] *Let's Talk Relationships: Nana's Pound Cake.* Narrated by Ronnie Johnson.

[4] *What You Thought You Lost.* Narrated by Judah Smith.

[5] *Don't Forget to Remember.* Narrated by Robert Madu.

Chapter 5

[1] *The Holy Bible.* New International Version. 1978. https://www.biblegateway.com.

[2] *Inner Peace.* Narrated by Erwin McManus.

Glue that Heals

[1] "The Japanese Art of Fixing Broken Pottery." Video. YouTube. Posted by BBC REEL,

August 5, 2020. *https://www.youtube.com/* watch?v=r9LMKGteoUU&list=WL&index=1.

2. Ibid.

Chapter 6

1 *The Holy Bible.* New International Version. 1978. *https://www.biblegateway.com.*

2 *Same Devils, New Levels.* Narrated by Steven Furtick.

3 Mumpower LiBasci, Sylina. "The Wounded Lion." *Chalkboard Reality* (blog). Entry posted April 3, 2017. *https://achalkboardreality.wordpress.com/2017 /04/03/the-wounded-lion/.*

4 *Same Devils, New Levels.* Narrated by Steven Furtick.

5 *Borrowed Confidence.* Narrated by Steven Furtick.

Chapter 7

1 *The Holy Bible.* New International Version. 1978. *https://www.biblegateway.com.*

2 Elwell, Walter A. "Entry for 'Clean, Unclean'". "Evangelical Dictionary of Theology". . 1997.

Chapter 8

1 *The Holy Bible.* New International Version. 1978. *https://www.biblegateway.com.*

2 *Great is Your Faithfulness.* Narrated by Louie Giglio.

Chapter 9

1 *The Holy Bible.* New International Version. 1978. *https://www.biblegateway.com.*

2 *Heart Rehab: That Was Toxic.* Narrated by Jerry Flowers.

3 *Heart Rehab: It Started in Childhood.* Narrated by Jerry Flowers.

4. *Get to the Good Part.* Narrated by Steven Furtick.

5 *Heart Rehab: That Was Toxic.* Narrated by Jerry Flowers.

Chapter 10

1 *The Holy Bible.* New International Version. 1978. *https://www.biblegateway.com.*

2 *Why Is It So Hard to Accept Myself.* Narrated by Steven Furtick.

3 *Between 2 Fires.* Narrated by Shawn Johnson.

4 *Healing from Shame.* Narrated by Craig Groeschel.

5 *I'm Going Out of My Mind.* Narrated by Steven Furtick.

Chapter 11

1 *The Holy Bible.* New International Version. 1978. https://www.biblegateway.com.

2 Scripture quotations are from the ESV® Bible (The Holy Bible, English Standard Version®), copyright © 2001 by Crossway, a publishing ministry of Good News Publishers. Used by permission. All rights reserved.

3 *Why I Went Off.* Narrated by Steven Furtick.

4 *Let's Talk Relationships: Nana's Pound Cake.* Narrated by Ronnie Johnson.

5 Brown, Brené. *DARING GREATLY: How the Courage to Be Vulnerable Transforms the Way We Live, Love, Parent and Lead.* London, England: Portfolio Penguin, 2013.

Chapter 12

1 *The Holy Bible.* New International Version. 1978. *https://www.biblegateway.com.*

2 *Running on Empty.* Narrated by Holly Furtick.

3 *Jesus on Trauma: Trauma and Identity.* Narrated by Judah Smith.

4 *I'm Not Ready for This.* Narrated by Holly Furtick.

5 *Demolition Day.* Narrated by Robert Madu.

Holes in Wholeness

1 "The Japanese Art of Fixing Broken Pottery." Video. YouTube. Posted by BBC REEL,

August 5, 2020.
*https://www.youtube.com/watch?v=r9LMKGte
oUU&list=WL&index=1.*

Chapter 13

1 Scripture quotations are from the ESV® Bible (The Holy Bible, English Standard Version®), copyright © 2001 by Crossway, a publishing ministry of Good News Publishers. Used by permission. All rights reserved.

2 *The Holy Bible.* New International Version. 1978. *https://www.biblegateway.com.*

3 *The Blessing of a Weight.* Narrated by Jeremy Foster.

4 *Take the Lid Off a Little.* Narrated by Steven Furtick.

5 *Running on Empty.* Narrated by Holly Furtick.

Chapter 14

1 *The Holy Bible.* New International Version. 1978. *https://www.biblegateway.com.*

2 *Men Like Trees.* Narrated by Robert Madu.

3 Ibid.

4 Desai, Unnati, Dr. "Scars: A Guide to Good Healing." *Nuffield Health,* May 14, 2021. *https://www.nuffieldhealth.com/article/scars-a-guide-to-good-healing.*

Chapter 15

[1] Scripture quotations are from the ESV® Bible (The Holy Bible, English Standard Version®), copyright © 2001 by Crossway, a publishing ministry of Good News Publishers. Used by permission. All rights reserved.

[2] "Takotsubo Cardiomyopathy." British Heart Foundation. Last modified January 2020. *https://www.bhf.org.uk/informationsupport/co nditions/cardiomyopathy/takotsubo-cardiomyopathy.*

[3] *Hosea: The Story of Redemption.* Narrated by Lisa Harper.

[4] *Shaped Not Scarred.* Narrated by Stephen Chandler.

[5] Center for Substance Abuse Treatment (US). Trauma-Informed Care in Behavioral Health Services. Rockville (MD): Substance Abuse and Mental Health Services Administration (US); 2014. (Treatment Improvement Protocol (TIP) Series, No. 57.) Chapter 3, Understanding the Impact of Trauma. Available from: *https://www.ncbi.nlm.nih.gov/books/NBK20719 1/*

[6] Ibid.

Chapter 16

[1] *The Holy Bible.* New International Version. 1978. *https://www.biblegateway.com.*

[2] *What You Call Small.* Narrated by Steven Furtick.

[3] *Protect the Vessel.* Narrated by Steven Furtick.

Chapter 17

[1] *The Holy Bible.* New International Version. 1978. *https://www.biblegateway.com.*

[2] *Miracle Mindset.* Narrated by Lisa Harper.

[3] Lewis, Danny. "Death Valley Bursts to Life with Rare 'Super Bloom.'" *Smithsonian Magazine*, February 23, 2016. *https://www.smithsonianmag.com/smart-news/death-valley-bursts-life-rare-super-bloom-180958194/*.

[4] *What God Left Out: Flatbread Faith*. Narrated by Steven Furtick.

[5] "There is a Cloud." Produced by Elevation Worship. *There is a Cloud*.

[6] Nichols, Morgan Harper. *All Along You Were Blooming*. N.p.: Zondervan, 2020.

Conclusion

[1] Scripture quotations are from the ESV® Bible (The Holy Bible, English Standard Version®), copyright © 2001 by Crossway, a publishing ministry of Good News Publishers. Used by permission. All rights reserved.

[2] *Timing Your Testimony*. Narrated by Steven Furtick.

School

About the Author

Mariah Miller is a sarcastic and compassionate middle school teacher who loves learning with her students. She lives in Denver where she enjoys a good hike and the gorgeous fall foliage. You can find her tackling a good DIY project on a Saturday or spending time with friends. She has had a love for writing since she was a teenager. Over the years she has filled over 25 journals with all the fun, messy, and crazy parts of life. She knows from personal experience that stories have the power to heal, and that is why she writes.

Thank You
For Reading My Book!

I really appreciate all of your feedback, and I love hearing what you have to say. I need your input to make the next version of this book and my future books better.

Please leave me an honest review on Amazon letting me know what you thought of the book.

Thanks so much!

Mariah